THE IMPORTANCE OF

Charlie Chaplin

These and other titles are included in The Importance Of biography series:

THE IMPORTANCE OF

Charlie Chaplin

by
Arthur Diamond

Lucent Books, P.O. Box 289011, San Diego, CA 92198-9011

Acknowledgments

Thanks to two mentors, Ralph Salisbury and William S. Wilson.
Your acuity and kindness will always be remembered.

Library of Congress Cataloging-in-Publication Data

Diamond, Arthur.
    The importance of Charlie Chaplin / by Arthur Diamond.
       p. cm.
    Includes bibliographical references and index.
    ISBN 1-56006-064-6
    1. Chaplin, Charlie, 1889–1977—Juvenile literature.
2. Motion picture actors and actresses—United States—
Biography—Juvenile literature. 3. Comedians—United States—
Biography—Juvenile literature. [1. Chaplin, Charlie, 1889–
1977. 2. Actors and actresses. 3. Comedians.] I. Title.
PN2287.C5D5   1995
791.43'028'092—dc20
[B]   94-23272
                                          CIP
                                          AC

Copyright 1995 by Lucent Books, Inc., P.O. Box 289011,
San Diego, California, 92198-9011

Printed in the U.S.A.

Dedication

To Alfred and Luly Kaufmann

Contents

Foreword

THE IMPORTANCE OF biography series deals with individuals who have made a unique contribution to history. The editors of the series have deliberately chosen to cast a wide net and include people from all fields of endeavor. Individuals from politics, music, art, literature, philosophy, science, sports, and religion are all represented. In addition, the editors did not restrict the series to individuals whose accomplishments have helped change the course of history. Of necessity, this criterion would have eliminated many whose contribution was great, though limited. Charles Darwin, for example, was responsible for radically altering the scientific view of the natural history of the world. His achievements continue to impact the study of science today. Others, such as Chief Joseph of the Nez Percé, played a pivotal role in the history of their own people. While Joseph's influence does not extend much beyond the Nez Percé, his nonviolent resistance to white expansion and his continuing role in protecting his tribe and his homeland remain an inspiration to all.

These biographies are more than factual chronicles. Each volume attempts to emphasize an individual's contributions both in his or her own time and for posterity. For example, the voyages of Christopher Columbus opened the way to European colonization of the New World. Unquestionably, his encounter with the New World brought monumental changes to both Europe and the Americas in his day. Today, however, the broader impact of Columbus's voyages is being critically scrutinized. *Christopher Columbus,* as well as every biography in The Importance Of series, includes and evaluates the most recent scholarship available on each subject.

Each author includes a wide variety of primary and secondary source quotations to document and substantiate his or her work. All quotes are footnoted to show readers exactly how and where biographers derive their information, as well as to provide stepping stones to further research. These quotations enliven the text by giving readers eyewitness views of the life and times of each individual covered in The Importance Of series.

Finally, each volume is enhanced by photographs, bibliographies, chronologies, and comprehensive indexes. For both the casual reader and the student engaged in research, The Importance Of biographies will be a fascinating adventure into the lives of people who have helped shape humanity's past and present, and who will continue to shape its future.

Important Dates in the Life of Charlie Chaplin

Charles Chaplin Jr. is born to Charles and Hannah Hill Chaplin on April 16 — **1889**

1901 — Charles senior dies at age thirty-seven after years of alcohol abuse

Hannah Chaplin, committed as a lunatic, is transferred from an infirmary to Cane Hill Asylum, where she remains until 1912 — **1903**

1907 — Begins work with the Karno Company

Signs contract with Keystone Film Company — **1913** / **1914**

1914 — Begins to appear in Keystone films; introduces the Little Tramp in *Mabel's Strange Predicament;* signs with Essanay for $1,250 per week to make fourteen films

Signs with Mutual Film Corporation for $10,000 per week, with a bonus of $150,000 — **1916**

1917 — Signs with First National Exhibitors' Circuit for salary exceeding $1 million per year

After two years of work, Chaplin releases *The Kid*, his first feature-length film — **1921**

1924 — Begins shooting *The Gold Rush*

Attends world premiere of *City Lights* in Los Angeles — **1931**

1936 — *Modern Times* is released; Chaplin marries costar Paulette Goddard

World premiere in New York of *The Great Dictator*, costarring Paulette Goddard — **1940**

1942 — Paulette Goddard is granted divorce from Chaplin

Chaplin marries Oona O'Neill — **1943**

1944 — Is indicted by federal grand jury on Mann Act charges involving actress Joan Barry (found not guilty two months later)

Joan Barry wins paternity suit against Chaplin — **1945**

1946 — Begins shooting of *Monsieur Verdoux*

Leaves for European publicity tour and is notified that his reentry permit has been rescinded; attends premiere of *Limelight* in London — **1952**

1953 — Moves into Manoir de Ban, in Vevey, Switzerland

Dies in his sleep at the family estate in Vevey, Switzerland, on December 25 — **1977**

A Tramp Is Born

In December 1913, after a second successful U.S. tour with the Karno Company, a British comedy troupe, English vaudeville comedian Charlie Chaplin felt optimistic about the future. The twenty-four-year-old Chaplin had already gained a reputation as one of England's finest clowns, acclaimed for his physical grace and his inventiveness, and also for his ability to create character. In the United States he had made a similar impression, and he had just signed a contract with the Keystone Film Company in Hollywood—a contract that offered him more money than he had ever made in his life, as well as the opportunity to bring his comedic gifts to the new medium, film.

Not long after beginning work at Keystone, though, Chaplin felt a little less sure of the move. After his arrival at the studio, he had been intimidated by the busy, sometimes frantic action resulting from three films being shot at the same time, on stages one next to the other. During his first few days, Chaplin had spoken little to anyone in producer-director Mack Sennett's troupe. And Sennett had not rushed to utilize his new star, either. Finally, in Chaplin's first appearance, in a film called *Making a Living*, he had not been impressive. He'd played an Englishman sporting a monocle and a handlebar mustache, and wearing a traditional vaudeville costume consisting of silk top hat, frock coat, checkered waistcoat, and polka-dot tie. Chaplin felt there was something wrong. There was something missing—the costume just hadn't inspired him. He knew he needed another outfit.

Charlie Chaplin in 1914, on the cusp of worldwide movie stardom.

In early February 1914, soon after his first film appearance, Chaplin visited the studio wardrobe to find something to wear for Sennett's next film. Trusting his instinct for comedy, he decided to try for a look of contrasts, and he picked out clothes and accessories with this idea in mind. He grabbed a pair of baggy pants, much too big for him. He put on a jacket that was too small, took a bowler hat that was small, too, and then picked out a bamboo cane. For shoes, he reached for a pair of oversize boots—they were so large he had to wear them on the wrong feet to keep them from falling off. Finally, he pasted on a small "toothbrush" mustache.

The well-known costume of the Little Tramp, the clothing of the beloved character most responsible for Chaplin's fame.

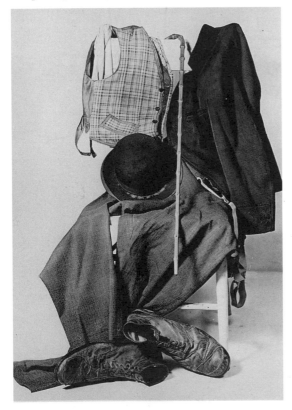

The size of the mustache, he knew, had an advantage—his facial expressions would not be obscured by it. "I had no idea of the character," he would later admit.

> But the moment I was dressed, the clothes and the make-up made me feel the person he was. I began to know him. . . . When I confronted Sennett I assumed the character and strutted about, swinging my cane and parading before him. Gags and comedy ideas went racing through my mind.[1]

Chaplin then took the stage, and the others assumed their places: Sennett in his director's chair, the cameramen behind their cameras, the other players in position on the set, which, for this scene, was a hotel lobby. Chaplin recalls what happened next:

> In all comedy business an attitude is most important, but it is not always easy to find an attitude. However, in the hotel lobby I felt I was an imposter posing as one of the guests, but in reality I was a tramp just wanting a little shelter. I entered and stumbled over the foot of a lady. I turned and raised my hat apologetically, then turned and stumbled over a cuspidor. Behind the camera they began to laugh.[2]

It began with the cameramen, that day on the Keystone set. Then Mack Sennett began to laugh. Word got around quickly, and the crews from the other sets came to watch. They all began laughing, too.

While the costume—in its parts and as a whole—had its origins in the English music hall, Chaplin's character was new. For one thing, it was complex—at once a gentleman and a bully, a cynic and an innocent. Also, the character's interactions with the world around him were not only complex, but wonderfully humorous. Finally, Chaplin was a superb mime, and this talent imbued the new character with a comedic grace that thrilled audiences.

The film, *Mabel's Strange Predicament*, was an immediate success. And the laughter that had begun that winter day in early 1914 continued throughout Chaplin's first year in pictures, then through his second and third years making short films. By then it was not just film audiences in America but people all over the world, gathered in the darkness of movie theaters everywhere, reading the opening titles in any number of languages, sitting back to take in the comic adventures of the Little Tramp. The character eventually "developed in both style and substance until he had evolved into a creation of humor and poignancy unmatched in film comedy."[3]

Charlie Chaplin would in time be acknowledged as perhaps the greatest comedian of all time; he would be applauded and respected for his great body of work as well as his personal courage in the face of Nazism and, later, McCarthyism—but he would always be loved as the Little Tramp.

Chaplin in his 1928 film, The Circus, *one of the comedian's many works hailed by audiences and critics alike.*

Chapter

1 A Dickensian Childhood

As a child performer, Charlie Chaplin was fascinated with and mimicked characters from the books of the great English novelist Charles Dickens. It was no wonder that he was attracted to Dickens's novels and their assortment of eccentric characters and dire social problems: young Chaplin's own life was straight out of a Dickens novel, with the same poverty, cruelty, heartbreak, and utter loneliness.

Charles Spencer Chaplin Jr. was born in England on April 16, 1889, the younger of two children of Charles and Hannah Chaplin. His first home, in the slums of South London, was in a part of the city called Walworth, which lay just across the Thames River from the working-class neighborhoods of Kensington and Lambeth. The landscapes of these three South London slum areas were dominated by factories, dilapidated buildings, and boardinghouses.

The slums where young Charlie grew up also had public houses, or taverns, to offer neighbors a break from their grim surroundings. The pubs, as they are called in England, serve food and drink, and used to feature aspiring performers trying out their acts on a one-night basis. Charlie's parents were performers and often

Walworth Road S. E.

A turn-of-the-century photo of Walworth, one of the London slums where Charlie spent his early years. Chaplin's parents made a living by performing in some of the slum's many taverns and music halls.

found work at the public houses. Sometimes, they appeared at a regional—or central—music hall.

London and the Music Halls

Music halls were very popular in England near the end of the nineteenth century. By 1886, there were 36 such theaters in London, and more than 230 throughout the rest of the country. The music halls were an offshoot of the great English stage tradition, and they featured vaudeville shows. In the United States during the late 1880s, this term applied to shows that featured song-and-dance acts, juggling, magic, drama, and comedy.

Audiences were composed of working-class people looking for an easy night of entertainment. These customers wanted broad humor—much of it on the racy side—a bit of drama and strong sentiment, then a return to broad and lively humor.

At the turn of the century, a vaudeville performer led a grueling life. Since work was very unpredictable, performers took advantage of every opportunity, even if it meant working several theaters in one evening. Because of the staggered performance times, an actor could sing at 8 P.M. in one theater, then change and hurry over to another playhouse for an appearance an hour later. The music hall performers did not have creative independence, nor did they have political individuality. Most performers were entirely at the beck and call of their agents and the theater owners.

Most performers had trouble enough just surviving. Charlie always remembered walking in the street with his mother one

Shows featuring juggling, song-and-dance acts, drama, magic, or comedy were called vaudeville, a popular form of entertainment in London music halls.

day when a ragged, dirty woman came up to them, asking for a handout. The beggar turned out to be Eva Lester, who had once drawn rave reviews for her brash singing style. Charlie was disgusted and frightened by this unfortunate woman with her shaven head and foul odor. But Hannah took Eva Lester by the arm, walked the former vaudeville star to the Chaplins' apartment, and cleaned her up.

The Chaplin Family

Charlie's mother, Hannah Hill Chaplin, was "petite and pretty, with a sympathetic and charming personality; she was liked

Charlie's mother Hannah was an aspiring singer. She was well-loved for her charming personality and kind, good nature.

by everyone for her kindness and good nature."[4] Hannah tried to be a singer. Known on the stage as Lily Harley, she had begun her career after marrying Charles, and in her brief career had had a few successful appearances in music halls.

Charles Chaplin Sr. composed and sang sentimental ballads. He had dark, sad eyes, and Hannah always said he looked like Napoleon. In contrast to Hannah, Charles had several good years in the music halls. He was considered a star. In 1898 he earned top billing at the New Empire Palace Theatre of Varieties in Leicester, one of the prominent locales for show business in London.

Charles and Hannah Chaplin had a difficult marriage. From the outset, the various pulls of their careers had divided them. Another difficulty was Charles's alcohol abuse, a main factor in the decline of many music hall performers. Finally, Charles and Hannah were unfaithful to each other. They separated in 1892, when Charlie was three and a half years old. "I was hardly aware of a father, and do not remember him having lived with us," recalled Charlie.[5]

Young Charlie was very close to his brother Sydney, four years older, who was born before Hannah's marriage to Charles senior. Sydney and Charlie would remain close throughout their lives. Without a father in the home, the two boys depended heavily on each other for love and support.

Charles Chaplin Sr. was a successful composer and singer. His alcohol abuse contributed to the failure of his marriage and the decline of his career.

The Pub

Chaplin's parents began their careers singing in London public houses, or pubs. In their book Chaplin: Genesis of a Clown, *Raoul Sobel and David Francis identify the pub as an essential part of community life for the poor of London.*

"As a cheaply hired meeting-place it had welcomed friendly societies, Sunday schools, burial clubs and trade unions. It always occupied a strategic position, such as a street corner or a point close by a railway station. Workmen could breakfast in it first thing in the morning and call in again on their way home at night. It was deliberately tricked out to seduce the passer-by. It boasted colorful signboards, elegant frosted glass, brilliant lamps and prettily arranged tables on the pavement outside, which in those days was alive with pedestrians. Even the stiff-backed Victorians could appreciate that, in a society starved of recreation, the pub was one of the few routes open to the working man by which he could escape the unredeemed squalor of his life. Its attraction was irresistible."

Terrible Circumstances

After Charles senior left the family, Hannah was supported for a while by her boyfriend, George Leo Dryden, known as Leo Dryden, a successful music-hall singer. The couple had a child, George Dryden Wheeler, who would later go by the name of Wheeler Dryden. After Wheeler's birth, Leo Dryden took care of Hannah's finances for a few months, but he never lived with her. Then one day, Leo came for a visit, suddenly snatched up the six-month-old baby, and disappeared.

Emotionally distraught over the apparent loss of her infant son, and with no financial support from Leo, Hannah now had to struggle to keep her family together. She worked constantly at dressmaking and at nursing (at that time, a person did not need many qualifications to be a nurse), and she also returned to the theaters to sing. At home, even though her children were forced to wear clothing stitched together from various threads and often went hungry, she made sure they spoke properly and practiced good manners.

Working constantly wore Hannah down. By the time Charlie was five, Hannah's voice, which was never strong, had given way to chronic laryngitis. One night, she appeared on stage before an audience of soldiers, who grew impatient with her failing voice and booed her into the wings. Many years later, Chaplin wrote: "I remember standing in the wings when Mother's voice cracked and went into a whisper; the audience began to laugh. . . . [T]he noise

The Old Lambeth Workhouse in London, a last resort for destitute families. Charlie and his brother Sydney lived three miserable weeks in a similar workhouse after their ill mother was sent to an infirmary.

increased until Mother was obliged to walk off the stage. . . . Mother's friends said something about letting me go in her place."[6]

When five-year-old Charlie walked onto the stage to face the hostile audience, the booing halted. Charlie quickly broke into a song, for Hannah had taught him to sing and dance, and at the age of four he had performed outside for tips. The soldiers responded favorably to the little boy's impromptu act, applauding and throwing coins onto the stage. Charlie went on to do a few impersonations, and again, the stage was strewn with money. It was his first performance on a public stage. Hannah Chaplin never performed in public again.

Destitution

The Chaplin family fell on hard times. They moved from three-room apartments to two rooms, to one, then to attics and basements. Hannah continued searching for jobs as a dressmaker and as a nurse, and she attended church for strength. She had to pawn the family belongings.

Charlie often danced, sang, and did impersonations in an effort to cheer her up. He and Sydney would greet their mother at the end of the day and dance for her or recite passages of plays, and she would momentarily forget about her troubles. Sometimes she took the boys to the window to watch people come and go, up and down the busy street, providing commentary to enhance the only entertainment she could afford. She would say she could tell that this one had had a difficult day on the job, because of the way he walked. If she saw a man go into a flower shop, she would try to predict what color flowers he would buy. Charlie always maintained that it was his mother who stimulated his own talent for creation of character.

But their poverty grew more severe, and Hannah's physical condition deteriorated. Suffering from acute headaches, she was admitted to the Lambeth Infirmary, a public hospital, where she stayed a full month in 1895. Charlie was sent off to stay with the Hodges family, distant relations of Hannah's who also lived in London. Homesick, Charlie grew distracted and barely attended the school he'd been enrolled in. He yearned for the day of reunion with Hannah and Sydney. Sydney spent most of the next eight months in the West Norwood Schools, which took in children of the poor.

Happily, the family was reunited by the spring of 1896. But Hannah, destitute, fell ill again and was soon readmitted to the infirmary. Once more, the Chaplin family life was shattered.

This time, Sydney and Charlie, now eleven and seven, were sent to Newington Workhouse. The workhouse was an institution in England. Created for the maintenance of the poor, it was the last place of refuge for families unable to provide for themselves. Here, men, women, and children worked hard at menial jobs during the day, often indoors and in miserable conditions, to earn food and shelter for the night.

It was a devastating experience for Hannah and her children. They could meet only during visiting hours; then they held hands and wept. The one thing that buoyed young Charlie was his relationship with his older brother. Sydney had enthusiasm and would soon display a drive to succeed in any way he could. Sydney had become the man of the family, and Charlie looked up to him with love.

The Family's Descent

The Chaplins' lives had begun a speedy downward spiral. On June 18, 1896—after three weeks at Newington Workhouse—Charlie and Sydney were transferred to

The Shame of Poverty

There was no respite from poverty for Hannah Chaplin and her sons. In My Autobiography, *Chaplin would remember the painful stigma attached to their condition.*

"Even the poorest of children sat down to a home-cooked Sunday dinner. A roast at home meant respectability, a ritual that distinguished one poor class from another. Those who would not sit down to Sunday dinner at home were of the mendicant [beggar] class, and we were that. Mother would send me to the nearest coffee-shop to buy a sixpenny dinner (meat and two vegetables). The shame of it—especially on Sunday! I would harry her for not preparing something at home, and she would vainly try to explain that cooking at home would cost twice as much."

Seven-year-old Charlie (third row, center) at the Hanwell boarding school for orphans and destitute children.

the Central London District Poor Law School at Hanwell, a boarding school for orphans and destitute children. At Hanwell, Charlie witnessed beatings of other children for misbehavior and was once severely beaten himself. In November, Sydney was transferred from the school to a training ship used to teach destitute boys to become crewmen; Charlie, now aged eight, was left behind and spent all the following year at Hanwell. There is little firm evidence of where Hannah was in 1897.

In January 1898, the London courts forced Charles Chaplin Sr. to take responsibility for his sons; Charles senior, how-

ever, asked that the boys be placed in the custody of their mother, thereby releasing himself from future financial responsibility. Sydney and Charlie were then reunited with Hannah.

For a few months, the little family enjoyed a quiet, close life in a number of dwellings, but in July, unable to fend for themselves, they returned to the workhouse. Though determined to remain strong and positive for her sons, Hannah suffered from mental illness, and in September 1898 she was sent from the workhouse to the infirmary, and then to a mental institution, the Cane Hill Asylum.

Life with Father

Two weeks after Hannah entered the asylum, the court again ordered Charles senior to take care of his sons. Charles, an alcoholic, lived with a thirty-year-old woman named Louise, who resented Sydney and Charlie. She made the brothers go on errands and clean the house. She locked Charlie out of the house. Once Charlie spent a whole Saturday without food, wandering the streets of London alone until midnight. When Charlie returned to the house, Louise, drunk, refused to let him in. Charles senior, hearing of this, knocked his girlfriend unconscious with a hairbrush. This didn't keep Louise from continuing to mistreat Charlie and Sydney. After the boys had spent two miserable months with Charles and Louise, the authorities intervened and returned the children to Hannah, who had just been discharged from the asylum. In early November 1898, the little family was again reunited. They lived now in a single rented room behind a pickle factory.

Hannah sent Charlie back to school, which distracted him from the strain of his family situation. He had never enjoyed school, which he had not attended regularly because of the family's difficulties, but now he began entertaining the class with comedic recitations, often of famous poems. Teachers and students alike appreciated him, and he began to look forward to going to school every morning. But school for Charlie ended abruptly in late November 1898 when, at age nine, he took a job with a popular traveling vaudeville troupe.

A Lancashire Lad

Persuaded by Charles Chaplin Sr., and with Hannah's assent, the manager of an act called the Eight Lancashire Lads hired Charlie as a member of the troupe, which performed all over England. The "lads"—five of whom were the children of the manager, William Jackson—were aged nine to sixteen. Mr. Jackson was a religious man and a former schoolteacher, and this pleased the parents of the children who were in the troupe. Hannah was also pleased because she would receive a regular allowance out of Charlie's salary.

The experience was a good one for Charlie—he made a little money while continuing his schooling, either in London or in small towns throughout the countryside. But the experience was hard. During his two years as a Lancashire Lad, Charlie was exposed to the grueling vaudeville schedule, which for him entailed clog dancing and comedy skits, performed perhaps twice or three times every night.

A Vulgar Cat

While the admiring Mr. Jackson allowed Charlie to perform as an acrobat and as an impersonator of Bransby Williams, a prominent reciter of monologues from the works of Dickens, it was as an animal

Chaplin was constantly adjusting to different homes and living situations. He once lived with his family in a house at Pownall Terrace (pictured).

that Charlie gave his most telling performance. The youthful troupe often filled in parts in larger productions, and in one of these young Charlie gave a memorable performance. The Lancashire Lads played the roles of various animals in a performance of *Cinderella*, given at the London Hippodrome at Christmastime in 1900. Charlie was assigned to play a cat. In this role, he sniffed the dog unexpectedly, then lifted his hind leg.

Charlie's performance drew gales of laughter—from everyone but the manager of the theater, who claimed that he would lose his license if the lord chamberlain, an important officer of Queen Victoria's household in charge of licensing all theaters and plays got wind of the vulgarity of the "cat." For the next performance Charlie played the role more conserva-

tively. In this small part, young Chaplin's ability to find the right chord to strike with the audience was a foreshadowing of the great comedic talent he would share with the world.

With Hannah

Charlie toured with the Eight Lancashire Lads for two years, but William Jackson became tired of Hannah's constant complaints that her son always looked weak and weary when he came home. Thus when Charlie was eleven, Jackson sent him back to his mother. Soon, Sydney joined them, fresh from several sea voyages and with money in his pocket. While the Chaplins lived a happy life for a while, dis-

Hannah's Influence

Raoul Sobel and David Francis, in their book Chaplin: Genesis of a Clown, *pointing to Chaplin's autobiography, note the influence of Hannah Chaplin on her son, an influence that would color his future relationships with women.*

"She emerges not as a person of real flesh and blood, but more like a wraith [ghost] not quite making real contact with either her son or the life around her. Chaplin never calls her 'my mother,' always 'Mother'—not a very positive way of expressing close and warm love. He seems to be standing aside, watching her plight, more concerned with his own sadness or grief of loneliness than with the plight itself . . . [in his later dealings with women] torn between his desperate need for love and his fear of loving in return, he wavered like a drunk man from woman to woman. . . . His ideal woman might possibly have been one who was mature and accommodating to his moods and obsessions, a mistress and mother substitute at the same time."

tracted from poverty, they learned that Charles senior was dying. In 1901 Charlie visited with his father for the last time. Passing a local tavern, Charlie had peeked in the window and spotted his father, whose body was swollen and clearly ruined by drink. Charles senior, happy to see his son, embraced him and asked him about himself and Hannah and Sydney. Three weeks later, on May 9, 1901, at age thirty-seven, Charles Chaplin Sr. was dead from cirrhosis of the liver.

For nearly two years, Charlie, desperate for money, avoided school and worked odd jobs. He found employment as a glass-blower, as a messenger boy, and as a doctor's helper. He worked at a stationer's store and then a printing shop. He found he liked working. "There was romance and adventure about getting out on those cold mornings, before daylight, and going to work, the streets silent and deserted."[7] During Charlie's spell at the printer's, he came down with the flu and had to return to the attic, where Hannah worked on a sewing machine, repairing clothes for a small income.

But again, Hannah's mind began to slip. By the spring of 1903 it was clear to Charlie that she was in trouble. But where could he turn? Sydney was at sea on what was to be his last voyage. Hannah grew un-responsive. She finally ignored her sewing machine, and soon the sweatshop that had loaned it to her came and repossessed it. Hannah didn't seem to care.

On Tuesday, May 5, Charlie came home and was informed by children in the street that his mother had gone insane. Thus at age fourteen, he had to take Hannah by the arm and lead her to the nearest infirmary. "As we left the house," he later recalled, "the neighbors and children were gathered at the front gate, looking on with awe."[8] At the infirmary, he had to confirm his mother's mental condition, explaining how she had been talking to imaginary people lately and how she tried to gain access to other people's lodgings. Charlie left the infirmary and went back to the attic, where he waited alone for four days until Sydney returned. The following week, Hannah was transferred to the Cane Hill Asylum once again.

The experience toughened young Charlie. It also gave him a lifelong empathy with those who lived in misery. He would forever carry with him the memories of childhood poverty—its sights, smells, tastes, and sounds. And to what would he owe his escape from these miserable beginnings? "Some of us are struck with good luck," he would contend, "and that is what happened to me."[9]

Chapter

2 Learning His Craft

In his autobiography, Charlie Chaplin states that he had wanted to be an actor since childhood. Toward the middle of 1903, living with his brother Sydney, he listed his name with one of London's most prestigious theatrical agencies and awaited a call for an audition. This was a bold move for Charlie, fourteen years old and wearing threadbare clothes, but he was determined to succeed.

Whether personal determination or simple luck, a call came almost immediately, and Charlie was given one role, as well as the opportunity to audition for another. His youth had qualified him to play a page boy in a production of *Sherlock Holmes* (1903–1905), scheduled to tour England for forty weeks. The second role portrayed Sammy, a "cheeky Cockney boy," in a melodrama called *Jim, a Romance of Cockayne*.[10] He was given the scripts and sent home.

Though without training, Charlie learned quickly. He had a little difficulty reading the material, but Sydney was able to help him. Charlie also practiced stage movement, something brand new to him, but he picked it up easily. By the time of his audition, he had learned both scripts well enough to impress one of the stars, H. A. Saintsbury. Chaplin would later recall: "After rehearsing a few scenes he was

astonished and wanted to know if I had acted before."[11]

While *Jim, a Romance of Cockayne*, did not win applause from the London critics, Charlie's performance did. One journalist described Chaplin as "a bright and vigorous child actor," of whom "great things" would be heard "in the near future."[12]

A London playbill for the highly successful production of Sherlock Holmes, *in which Chaplin played the small role of Billy the page boy.*

While working on Sherlock Holmes *Chaplin fell in love with Marie Doro, one of the show's stars. Their romance ended when Doro moved to America to pursue a film career.*

Charlie was pleased by the praise and got ready for rehearsals of *Sherlock Holmes*.

During the next four years, Charlie established himself as a recognized actor of West End, the theater district of London. He was known mainly for the small role of Billy the page boy in the highly successful *Sherlock Holmes*, which continued its run in London and throughout England. During this time, Sydney first worked as a bartender, then joined Charlie on a tour of *Sherlock Holmes*, much to Charlie's delight. The two brothers knew now, with their mother in a fragile mental state, that they must watch over each other.

While on tour, they got a letter from Hannah with the news that she had been released from the hospital. When the brothers returned to London, they lived briefly with their mother in an apartment over a barbershop. Then it was time for the brothers to go on tour again.

The *Sherlock Holmes* run came to an end, however, and teenaged Charlie was out of work. For almost a year, he used up his savings on drink, food, and women. "I was a worshipper of the foolhardy and the melodramatic, a dreamer and a moper, raging at life and loving it," he recalled in his autobiography.[13] He had also fallen in love with Marie Doro, one of the stars of the show, and now, with Doro returning to America for a film career, Charlie moped and mourned his loss.

In March 1906 Hannah had a relapse and was sent back to the hospital, then to the asylum, where a doctor concluded that she was "a Lunatic and a proper person to be taken charge of and detained under care and treatment. . . . She is very strange in manner and quite incoherent. She dances and sings and cries by turns."[14] Hannah would have to be looked after for the rest of her life.

A New Opportunity

Fortunately, Sydney, now twenty years old, provided an opportunity for his unemployed brother. In March 1906, Sydney had gotten a role in a sketch called *Repairs*, written by popular author and playwright Wal Pink, and he helped Charlie get hired for a role. Charlie played a plumber's assistant in a sketch featuring an aggressive union agitator, played by Sydney, who tried to get the dim-witted, inept plumbers to strike.

Charlie stayed with the show, which was moderately successful, until May 1906, when he found a role in a popular sketch called *Casey's Court Circus,* featuring comedian Will Murray. Murray played Mrs. Casey, an elderly lady who clowned around in an alley, accompanied by several juvenile comedians trying jointly to produce a kind of circus.

Recognizing Charlie's ability, Murray gave him a role in a second sketch, contrived to mock a strange celebrity of the time, Dr. Walford Bodie. An electrician by trade, Bodie had taken to the music hall stage as a magician and ventriloquist, claiming to be a fabulous healer, in fact "[t]he most remarkable man on Earth, the great healer, the modern miracle worker."[15] Among other miracles, he claimed to have used hypnosis to cure many paralyzed patients. Some people thought him a great healer, some a great fake. But he was clearly a great showman, dressed in a frock coat and a silk hat, his waxed mustache curling up at the ends.

Charlie had never seen Bodie on stage. But with Murray's help, the young mime was able to reproduce a number of mannerisms peculiar to Bodie, including the way he walked and turned. These Charlie practiced at great length, both alone in front of a mirror and later with the other members of the troupe. Not-surprisingly, Chaplin was an immediate hit with his impersonation. Said Will Murray in recollection, "he 'got' the audience right away with 'Dr. Bodie.'"[16]

When the *Casey's Court Circus* tour ended in July 1907, Charlie was again out

Audiences loved Chaplin's impersonation (pictured) of Dr. Walford Bodie, a celebrity showman who claimed to be "the most remarkable man on Earth."

of work. He searched for three months until landing a job with a traveling troupe where Sydney was already employed. The engagement with this organization, run by a man named Fred Karno, marked the beginning of Charlie's most important acting apprenticeship yet.

The Karno Company

Although Fred Karno had originally thought Sydney's little brother too serious and moody for comedy, he was won over during the audition by Charlie's miming and "his delicate dexterity."[17]

At this time, the Karno Company was one of the most prominent vaudeville companies in England. A one-time plumber, Fred Karno had been a member of a vaudeville troupe years before and, with a little bit of capital, had created the Fun Factory, where he built sets, created costumes, and trained his contracted comedians to perform original silent, slapstick routines that became popular throughout England. At the height of his success, Karno had thirty troupes working for him in England, continental Europe, and North America.

Charlie's early roles were small, though he did a lot with them. In one of his first roles, in a sketch called *Stiffy the Goaltender*, Charlie played a comic villain trying to bribe Stiffy to throw the game. Dressed in a silk top hat and a cloak, Charlie entered the stage with his back to the audience, appearing—from the back—to be graceful and refined in his movements. Then he turned around to reveal a big crimson

nose. After the audience's laughter subsided, Charlie proceeded to trip over his own cane and then collide with a few

In 1907 Charlie became a member of the Karno Company, a large, successful vaudeville company in England.

Chaplin in 1909. Despite his success as a performer with the Karno Company, many of the troupe members found Chaplin unsociable and unlikable.

more props. Offstage, the lead comedian, veteran comedian Harry Weldon, voiced his displeasure with the younger man's success, claiming that Chaplin was stealing the laughs. But Karno was quite pleased with his new actor.

Chaplin's Talents

It was clear to Fred Karno that Chaplin had special talents. For one thing, the young actor had a gift for mimicry. He could watch a person walking down the street, pick out a few significant and detailed characteristics—the walk, the tilt of the shoulders, a repeated hand movement—

and present a caricature of that person. It is likely that Chaplin's early attempts to cheer Hannah Chaplin by impersonating others had developed this ability.

He was also gifted at pantomime—the expression of ideas and thoughts by using the face and body alone. This art is one of the most difficult in the acting world, for the artist must make his or her intentions clear without saying a word. Chaplin's physical grace, witnessed in pantomime, was wonderful to watch. In one famous movement, which he seems to have picked up from Will Murray, he turned a corner at top speed, with the inside leg hopping in place, the outside leg up and parallel to the ground, quickly to come down in the new direction he was off in. "Chaplin's grace of movement and variety of expression made his colleagues appear a gang of bumpkins."[18]

Charlie was already a seasoned performer by the time he landed his job with Karno; still, he learned a great deal over the next six years. Karno had developed the technique of introducing a touch of sentiment during the comedy on stage. For example, when one character hit another, the aggressor always wore an expression of sympathy or regret for his actions for a few moments after striking the blow—Karno rightly perceived that this bit of decency created a connection with the audience.

Also, Karno taught his comedians to vary the pace of comedy, and to integrate the unexpected; that is, if a performer did not expect a pie in the face, neither would the audience, and this would make the scene that much more humorous. Later, Charlie Chaplin would mark his own films with sentiment and by varying the pace of the action.

Chaplin learned much from other Karno troupe members, too. Fred Kitchen, a comedian as well as a mime, taught Chaplin a series of falls and back kicks that would be identified with Chaplin. Kitchen also taught the younger man the special trick of throwing a cigarette back over the shoulder and kicking it up in the air with the heel of the shoe. Chaplin may have picked up his shuffling walk for the Little Tramp character from Kitchen's own curious shuffling gait.

A Sensitive Young Man

During the years 1908–1913, Chaplin gained acclaim for his comedy performances in the Karno Company. While Chaplin rose to the top, however, other performers in the troupe were not impressed. Of course, the man he had overshadowed back in the *Stiffy the Goaltender* sketch had less-than-glowing comments for Charlie, recalling that "although Karno had such a high opinion of Chaplin, no one else in the company paid him much attention but regarded him as one of the [junior members]."[19] Karno himself recalled Chaplin's lack of popularity with others in the troupe. "He wasn't very likable. I've known him to go whole weeks without saying a word to anyone in the company . . . on the whole he was dour [gloomy] and unsociable."[20]

If indeed "dour and unsociable," Chaplin was also sensitive and romantic. He fell in love again, and it colored his life. The object of his infatuation was fifteen-year-old Hetty Kelly, who danced in an act that played on the same bill as the Karno troupe. Chaplin would later de-

scribe her as "a slim gazelle, with a shapely oval face, a bewitching full mouth, and beautiful teeth."[21] He met her several times, and each time he was unable to keep from confessing his complete and total love for her. This confession frightened the young dancer away, and the relationship ended abruptly. However, Charlie's memory of his intense feelings always stayed with him.

Though hurt by the experience, Charlie did not allow it to interfere with his work. In 1909 he was given a prominent role as the drunk in Karno's sketch called *The Mumming Birds*. As the show begins, a young female usher is escorting a boy and

In The Mumming Birds *sketch, Chaplin played an obnoxious drunk who continually interrupts the show with his antics.*

Chaplin (center) with the Karno troupe en route to New York City to kick off their 1910 American tour.

his uncle to their theater seats. All of a sudden, a drunk is seated in the side box adjacent to the stage. The drunk is, of course, Charlie. He drunkenly peels off his gloves. In the words of author and mime Dan Kamin, "He then tried to light a cigarette by pressing it against an electric bulb, thus introducing one of the most pervasive gag devices of his films, treating one object as if it is another."[22] When offered a lit match by a boy in a nearby box seat, Chaplin reaches too far and falls forward out of the box and right onto the stage. During the course of the show, the action is continually interrupted by the drunk. Most crowds loved the joke of the "show-within-the-show" and Chaplin's masterful pantomime—though some audiences, unable to perceive that the drunk was part of the act—

grew upset and even hostile toward Chaplin's character!

To America

In 1910 Fred Karno scheduled an American tour of his London troupe, and Charlie arrived with the other players in New York City in the autumn of that year. He was greeted by Alf Reeves, the troupe's stateside manager. Chaplin found New York frightening by day, with its noise and fast pace, and its unending waves of people marching up and down the sidewalks under the shadows of the great skyscrapers. But the city came alive to him at night, when people were more relaxed and strolled about, seeking conversation and entertainment. He grew to love America because it was a classless society, where treatment of the individual depended on how much money a person had, not what class a person was born into. While successful back in London, Chaplin had felt looked down upon by the upper classes because of his poverty-stricken beginnings.

A New Medium

By the time Chaplin first arrived in America in 1910, audiences loved the dance hall as a form of entertainment, but they were also fascinated by a relatively new entertainment medium: the motion-picture film.

Motion pictures had been in existence—and constantly evolving—for about fifteen years. Thomas Edison's invention, the Kinetoscope, introduced in New York in 1894, allowed one to view film in a small box, like a peep show. The kinetograph, or camera, weighed nearly a ton,

Audiences flocked to nickelodeons to see a new form of entertainment that was sweeping America—the motion-picture film.

and events had to be brought to it for filming. In late 1895 Louis and Auguste Lumière of Lyons, France, produced the cinematograph, an improvement over Edison's machine. By projecting filmed

Desperately Shy

Stanley Jefferson, who would later become Stan Laurel in the comedy team Laurel and Hardy, had this to say about Chaplin in Chaplin: His Life and Art.

"To some of the company I know he appeared stand-offish and superior. He wasn't, he wasn't at all. And this is something a lot of people through the years don't know or refuse to believe about Charlie: he is a very, very shy man. You could even say he is a desperately shy man. He was never able to mix easily unless people came to him and volunteered friendship or unless he was among people who didn't know him. Then he wasn't so shy."

images onto a screen before an audience, the cinematograph liberated motion pictures from the one-on-one constraints of the peep show. Later that year the Lumiéres presided over the first public film show in Paris; the following year the brothers had public film showings in London, Vienna, New York, Bucharest, Egypt, India, Japan, and Australia. In 1903 Edwin Porter's film *The Great Train Robbery* met with tremendous success and initiated the building throughout the country of nickelodeons, the earliest motion-picture theaters. In 1907, there were five thousand nickelodeons in the United States. (Although the name "nickelodeon" was later used for small, coin-operated motion-picture machines, it originally described a theater where one paid a nickel

for a screen program with piano accompaniment.)

The success of the nickelodeons led to the establishment of movie palaces. Here, in opulent settings, the latest films were shown. The dominant figure on the scene in 1910 was David Wark (D. W.) Griffith, who, through his company Biograph, experimented as a film director and created "stars" to exploit the financial success of his films.

In America

In 1910, while Chaplin fell in love with America, New York audiences were unimpressed by the Karno troupe's show. Titled *The Wow-Wows*, the sketch centered around some summer campers' attempts to join a fellow camper's secret society. It featured jokes that just were not funny. Chaplin, though, stood out, as a reviewer in the influential entertainment paper *Variety* observed: "Chaplin will do all right for America, but it is too bad that he didn't first appear in New York with something with more in it than this piece."[23]

With time, the troupe managed to make their piece more acceptable to New York audiences and reviewers, but it was still a disappointment. However, when the Karno players reworked a few established routines into a new one, they received much more favorable attention. The new routine incorporated, among other things, the drunk in the box seat so prominent in *The Mumming Birds*. Chaplin, again, was singled out by reviewers for his comic performance.

With critical acclaim finally theirs, the Karno troupe left New York and em-

Pioneer film director and producer D. W. Griffith helped to create "movie stars" of many of the actors that appeared in his films.

Charlie shared a very close relationship with his brother Sydney, who is pictured here with his wife Minnie, a Karno Company actress.

barked on a twenty-week, three-shows-per-day tour of the country, and Charlie at first found it exciting to tour the United States. He stopped in Chicago, Minneapolis, Denver, and Seattle. He was greatly impressed by the well-dressed men and women in the red-light district of Butte, Montana. He admired the wide streets of Salt Lake City. He did not think much, though, of Los Angeles—the city where he was soon to make his fortune. Continuing his loner habits, he read incessantly and practiced his violin and his cello, both of which he played left-handed. After one and a half years on tour, though, Chaplin was ready for a break.

After completing their highly successful first American tour, Chaplin and the others sailed back to England, arriving in June 1912. Sydney's life had changed: he had married one of the Karno Company actresses, and, shortly afterward, he had

also given up the apartment he and Charlie had shared for a time after Hannah's move to the asylum. This upset Charlie, who felt robbed of the safe haven he'd had before leaving England. For the first time in his life, he felt distant from his brother—their relationship had changed. For Hannah, though, nothing had changed: she remained mentally unbalanced. Now that the brothers could afford it, they moved her to a private nursing home in London.

Chaplin and the company sailed back to America in October 1912 for a new Karno tour. In America, audiences out West continued to be impressed by Charlie Chaplin's performances. In Butte, Montana, a rugged mining town, one reviewer wrote favorably of *A Night in an English Music Hall* (formerly *The Mumming Birds*), exclaiming that Chaplin had proved himself as "one of the best pantomime artists ever seen. His falls in and out of the boxes are wonderful, and were he not a skilled acrobat, he would break his neck."[24] After the tour, the Karno troupe played in New York, then went west again.

A Telegram

During the Karno troupe's second tour, Charlie was told that a telegram awaited him in New York. He thought the message was to notify him that a relative had died, and he left the Karno Company in Kansas City on November 28, 1913. In New York, though, he was relieved to learn that there was no death in the family. And he was excited to discover that the telegram was an offer to work in the motion-picture industry.

Chapter

3 The First Year in Films

In 1913 Charlie Chaplin agreed to begin working with Mack Sennett's Keystone Film Company. According to his contract, Chaplin was engaged "as a moving picture actor to enact roles in the moving picture productions" of Keystone.[25]

While Keystone offered him $150 a week to appear in up to three films a week—twice his salary from Karno—Chaplin did not think Keystone had done much promising work. The studio had produced, in the words of Chaplin biographer Roger Manvell, "knockabout comedies," which Chaplin thought were "rough and lacking in finesse."[26]

The Sennett Style

More accurately, Keystone produced slapstick, a physical kind of comedy, with exaggerated gestures involving frenzied motions. Inanimate objects, like chairs, cars, ladders, and rugs, became the performers' sources of frustration. These movies had a sense of organized chaos about them, and usually they ended with a wild chase scene, entailing even more chaos and motion. The adjective *slapstick* derived from the device used by the buffoon character in a pantomime to make a

very loud noise—similar to a slap—without injuring the actor supposedly struck by the blow.

Of his company's films, Mack Sennett said, "Our specialty was exasperated dignity and the discombobulation [confusion] of Authority."[27] To create this

In 1913 Mack Sennett offered Chaplin a job with his Keystone Film Company doing slapstick comedy.

specialty, Sennett established a repertory company composed of animals and comics, with the settings representative of America at the early years of the century. His most successful comedy films featured the famous Keystone Kops, a team of comic actors who, as a squadron of policemen, played out a series of frantic chase scenes in hotel lobbies, at railroad stations, in hardware stores, amid earthquakes, and in burning buildings. A trademark of the Keystone Kops films was the custard pie in the face—the victim tended to be either a figure of authority or someone who was "a little too much on his or her dignity."[28]

The Fledgling Film Industry

The fast-paced growth and astonishing success of Keystone mirrored the popularity of the fledgling film industry. The public had developed an insatiable appetite for the new medium, especially for films of the kind put out by Sennett. For working-class viewers—the principal audiences of motion pictures—Sennett's films were more than a distraction from their dreary lives; the films were, in a way, an affirmation. "Life was nasty, brutish and short for most working people at this time; and the cinema . . . had reflected this brutality from the start."[29]

In their first year alone, Sennett set up shop in New York, filming on the city streets with illegally purchased cameras. Then, as demand for Keystone's short films grew, the company moved to Los Angeles and for the first time worked out of a studio. Keystone made 140 comedies in the first year, and the money flowed in so fast, boasted Sennett, that "my fingers ached from trying to count."[30] By the time he met Chaplin, Sennett was a multimillionaire, producing and directing films in Hollywood.

Sennett's most popular films featured the physical comedy of the Keystone Kops, a squadron of policemen involved in a series of chaotic chase scenes.

The Studio System

In the beginning, Hollywood stressed the value of the film companies over any individual performers. When Chaplin joined Keystone, it was the corporate name that the owners of the film corporations wanted foremost in the public's eye. Thus performers did not even receive screen credit—they were, after all, film company products: Florence Lawrence had been known as "the Biograph girl," for example, and Florence Turner was "the Vitagraph girl."

Many performers desired anonymity, too: motion pictures were still a novelty, and their primary purpose was to satisfy the entertainment cravings of the masses. "The movies" were not an acceptable art form, like stage drama. Many actors who accepted film roles did not want to ruin their chances for success in the legitimate theater by being identified with the less prestigious medium.

At age twenty-four, however, Chaplin did not want anonymity. With Keystone, besides working for a year in the new medium at twice his earlier salary, with none of the dreary, routine touring, he recognized great potential for publicity. By appearing in motion pictures, he could be seen by more people in a night than he could in a year of touring with Karno. He expected to become an international star within a year or so.

Lost and Abandoned

In December 1913, Chaplin joined Mack Sennett at the Keystone studio. After sit-

Often seen as film company products, early movie actors received little individual recognition. Actress Florence Turner (seated) was known as "the Vitagraph Girl" because she worked for the Vitagraph film company.

ting on the sidelines for several days, Chaplin finally received a nod from Sennett. He played the villain in a film called *Making a Living*, directed by one of Sennett's studio employees, Henry Lehrman. Chaplin wore a frock coat and a top hat, as well as a monocle and a droopy handlebar mustache. He performed some funny "business," especially with a large and unrestrained cuff which kept rolling down his arm and around his walking cane. In the reviews, he was cited as "a comedian of the first water [degree], who acts like one of Nature's own naturals."[31]

But the film, released in February 1914, was a flop, and Chaplin was angry. In the edited version, many of what Chaplin thought were clever, even ingenious gags, did not appear. He was convinced that Lehrman had edited his innovative work out of the film as revenge for the many suggestions and contrary opinions the new hire had voiced during the filming.

The Little Tramp

Soon after the wrapup of *Making a Living*, Chaplin received orders from Sennett to find a new costume for the next film. Working on intuition, he pulled together an odd assortment of clothes from the wardrobe department, including baggy trousers, oversized black shoes, a derby, and a cane. In this outfit, he appeared before Sennett, who gave his immediate approval.

According to scholars, Chaplin's first appearance as the Little Tramp was in the film called *Mabel's Strange Predicament*, starring Keystone comedienne Mabel Normand. The action revolves around a bedroom mix-up—one of Sennett's standard plot devices. Chaplin, in his tramp getup, plays a slightly drunk man in a hotel lobby. He proceeds to become entangled in a dog's leash, take some falls, and flirt with every passing female before fastening on Mabel, who, dressed in a nightgown, has locked herself out of her hotel room. Charlie chases her lecherously, then is embroiled in a confrontation between Mabel, her boyfriend, the man under

Crude and Vulgar

When Chaplin came to work for Mack Sennett, Keystone was one of the most popular motion-picture studios. Popular, though, does not always mean good, and in Classics of the Silent Screen, *Joe Franklin offers strong opinions about the quality of films put out by the Sennett studio.*

"The thing that impresses me most about Chaplin is what remarkable strides he made in his early years. The initial Keystones, made under Mack Sennett, were often unutterably crude and vulgar. The humor consisted of everyone running around at top speed, falling down on the slightest provocation, and delivering as many kicks to the posterior as the footage would allow. I am forever baffled by those historians who find a 'grace' and 'poetry' in the early Sennetts. They provided valuable training ground for a number of top comics, both players and directors, in their formulative years, and are not to be despised. They played a valuable role, and some were even very good. But the great Sennetts—and the great Chaplins—all came later."

Chaplin with Mabel Normand in Mabel's Strange Predicament, *the first film in which Chaplin appeared as the Little Tramp. The character was an immediate hit.*

whose bed Mabel finds herself, and the man's jealous wife. Charlie gets in the way of most of the blows exchanged by the other parties.

Chaplin's performance in *Mabel's Strange Predicament* had a great effect on Sennett. He was so impressed with Charlie's gags in the hotel lobby that he let the scene run for the full minute of the take, despite the director's objections.

Chaplin's next appearance—again as the Little Tramp—was in a five-minute entertainment that takes place at an amusement park. The film, *Kid Auto Races at Venice*, was directed by Henry Lehrman and released in February 1914. Here Charlie, in his tramp outfit, keeps popping out in front of the cameraman, who is trying to film the races. Chaplin thought of this simple "plot" after remembering a carnival procession captured by the camera of a newsreel photographer who was constantly distracted by a fat man in the crowd, who kept making grand gestures with his hands. In this film, Chaplin inter-

rupts the director, Henry Lehrman, repeatedly, waving his hands maniacally and chasing wildly after the children's cars. He even turns to Lehrman and sticks his tongue out at him. Again, the film met with great success.

Fighting the System

The next several films featuring Charlie's new character were similar to the first one, and they were successful. In these early films, the Tramp was mainly a villain or a buffoon, notable for his ability to deposit a well-aimed kick to someone's rear end or knock down an opponent with a wild punch to the chin. The Tramp also excelled in sliding, tumbling, and falling. His character was more or less one-dimensional, and clearly not a focus of audience sympathy. Sennett admits that Chaplin's character was at this stage "a real vagabond, a compound . . . of cruelty,

The Little Tramp's second appearance was in Kid Auto Races at Venice. *In the film, the tramp repeatedly pops out in front of the camera, frustrating the director who is trying to film the races.*

venality, treachery, larceny and lechery."[32] Chaplin himself offered a now-famous sketch of the character:

> You know this fellow is many-sided, a tramp, a gentleman, a poet, a dreamer, a lonely fellow, always hopeful of romance and adventure. He would have you believe he is a scientist, a musician, a duke, a polo-player. However, he is not above picking up cigarette-butts or robbing a baby of its candy. And, of course, if the occasion warrants it, he will kick a lady in the rear—but only in extreme anger![33]

While Chaplin's first performances were greeted warmly by critics and audiences, his attitude caused difficulties among the directors. Chaplin made four more films with Henry Lehrman and one with another veteran director, George

Nichols, and he fought with both men. He alienated everyone on the set when he argued with Mabel Normand, appointed by Sennett to be Chaplin's next director. Normand, who happened to be romantically involved with Sennett, took repeated abuse from Chaplin, who objected to her creative suggestions. After a particularly nasty fight, Chaplin left the studio. Sennett was furious. Chaplin went home thinking he would be fired.

The next day, though, Chaplin was in for a surprise. At the studio, Sennett and Normand expressed their regret at having upset him. The meeting was pleasant, and Chaplin agreed to finish the film he had been at work on. Only later did he find out that Sennett had orders from his East Coast distributors for more Chaplin films. Chaplin's first films had sold extremely well.

Learning to Direct

It became clear early on that Chaplin was not one to take direction. He had to be given free rein to decide what would work and what wouldn't. Chaplin needed to be in control of his own efforts. Mack Sennett said that Chaplin had once asked him, "If you want somebody to pull all of the old gags, why did you hire me?"[34]

Seeking more creative control for himself, Chaplin insisted on learning how to work behind the camera as well as in front of it. But by directing himself in his own films, Chaplin would come into direct conflict with Keystone's publicity system, which promoted the Keystone name over that of any of its individual stars. Chaplin would be in competition with his employer for public recognition. But since his first few films had been quite successful, Sennett, in an effort to keep his new star happy, agreed to let him learn to direct.

Without ceasing to fulfill his contractual obligations as a performer, Chaplin spent his first months at Keystone watching and learning how to direct and use a camera. For example, he had to remember that if a performer exited toward the camera, the very next scene, with the performer reentering, had to be shot with the performer's back to the camera. Also, he had to learn how to position a camera—when to have a close-up and when a long shot was preferable. There were other basics to learn too, such as how to keep an actor from stepping outside the range of the camera and how to edit.

Finally, having convinced Sennett and others at the studio that his own brand of pantomime, though slower than that of the Keystone Kops, was just as much ap-preciated by audiences, Chaplin was allowed to star in and direct his own films. At this time, New York was requesting more and more films—the demands by audiences for entertainment couldn't be met. By May of that first year, Chaplin had won his battle for independence and enjoyed complete creative control of the films he was to star in. As an enticement calculated to persuade Sennett, Chaplin put his money where his mouth was. He had managed to save $1,500 and promised to give it back to the studio if his own efforts lost money.

Chaplin never had to part with his $1,500—his first effort, *Caught in the Rain*, was a success; in fact, it was one of the most successful shorts produced by Keystone up to that time. The story is simple:

Chaplin in the editing room. Not one to take direction easily, Chaplin persuaded Sennett to give him complete creative control over his own films.

His New Job, *one of Chaplin's first efforts as star and director. Chaplin's first films further developed the Little Tramp character and were a huge success with audiences.*

Charlie flirts with a married lady in a hotel and eventually gets thrown out the window, into the rain. It is not much of a plot, but Chaplin's control as director is evident. He uses far fewer titles (now called subtitles—explanatory words and phrases displayed on the screen) than the average Keystone film, preferring to let the film's action tell the story and generate humor. Also, choice bits of virtuoso comedy are kept in—any director in the strict Keystone style, fearing slackness, would probably have edited them out.

In 1914 Chaplin made a total of thirty-five two-reelers (a two-reeler lasted half an hour) for Keystone, most of them in his role as the Little Tramp. The films were made quickly, some at breakneck speed: the one-reeler *Twenty Minutes of Love* was reportedly shot in a single afternoon. The average time for production for a two-reeler was about a week.

While Chaplin's first films under Sennett's supervision made the comedian appear more or less one-dimensional and unsympathetic, when he himself assumed control, the custard pies and the grand finale chase scenes that figured prominently in the Keystone Kops films were omitted. There was still plenty of slapstick, however, including wild chases that were often quite violent. Chaplin's character engaged in much kicking and pin-sticking, as well. He was on the receiving end of sharp blows with blunt instruments, including an ironing board in *His Trysting Place.* And he took some remarkable falls— in *His Favorite Pastime*, he tumbles head over heels from a staircase onto a sofa and lands upright, still smoking a cigarette.

There were wonderful sight gags in these films. In *A Film Johnnie*, Chaplin pulls a hose away from his soaked face, twists his ear, and spurts a stream of water from his

The Keystone World

In his biography entitled Chaplin: His Life and Art, *David Robinson describes the source of Mack Sennett's Keystone brand of comedy.*

"Keystone films derived from vaudeville, circus, comic strips, and at the same time from the realities of early twentieth-century America. It was a world of wide, dusty streets with one story clapboard houses, grocery and hardware stores, dentists' surgeries and saloon bars; kitchens and parlours; the lobbies of cheap hotels; bedrooms with iron beds and rickety washstands; railroad tracks and angular automobiles that were just overtaking the horse and buggy; men in bowler hats and heavy whiskers; ladies in feathered hats and harem skirts; spoiled children and stray dogs. The stuff of comedy was wild caricature of the ordinary joys and terrors of daily life."

mouth. The film *Twenty Minutes of Love* finds him so wistfully distracted by a couple necking in the park that he puts his arms amorously around a nearby tree. When posing as royalty in *Caught in the Cabaret,* he absently rests one foot on the opposite knee, only to discover a hole in his shoe; quickly he takes his hat off and hangs it on the toe.

Developing a Style

Chaplin was arriving at a way to make his films. He found that he preferred to work with an undeveloped script, a method used by Sennett. The undeveloped script, which gave only the bare bones of a plot, and no dialogue, allowed for much spontaneity and ingenuity—areas in which Chaplin excelled. He took his inspiration

from what he perceived at the moment, whether it was another performer, a set, a prop, or a story in a newspaper. Something would trigger a direction in his mind, and he'd pursue it, always intent on making the most of comic possibilities.

With Chaplin in charge, the films changed. For one thing, the unceasing, breathless action slowed down so that attention focused more on the development of character—another area Chaplin excelled in.

Chaplin began to experiment. In his autobiography he talked of having the Tramp skating in a rink, wreaking havoc by dodging and dashing and shooting between the other skaters' legs, then walking off the ice to a far seat in the background. At that point, the camera takes a long shot of the rink and the scene dissolves into chaos, with the Tramp visible far in the back. In this way, the audience gets the sense of the Tramp overseeing his "creation"—the chaos of the rink—and the audience sees it with him. A close-up of the Tramp would not have made as powerful an effect.

Popularity

Within a year after his debut in the cinema, Chaplin was an acknowledged success in American films. Chaplin biographer David Robinson states that while we look back at the Keystone films and see their roughness and crudity, to the American public at that time, "they arrived like rockets."[35]

Chaplin's audience, like Sennett's au-

Chaplin's comedic style provided his mostly working-class audiences with a welcome release from the harsh realities of life.

dience, was drawn primarily from the working class, much of which was composed of recently arrived immigrants. Eric Rhode notes that in general, the cinema "was to be a desperately needed consolation and source of knowledge to the poor, the illiterate and to immigrant communities (as in America) unable to speak the native language."[36] Rhode supplies an explanation for Chaplin's great popularity:

> It was probably the qualities which we may now think of as defects which won Chaplin his public: the meanness of his settings, especially, and the ugliness of his actions—whoever thwarts the tramp's wishes, however slightly, tends to be rewarded with punches and kicks. His working-class audiences lived among similar degradations— and life in the trenches was no improvement. They must have found in these comedies an identification and release from resentment they could not have found elsewhere.[37]

Audiences were especially grateful just then to be entertained by the Chaplin shorts, for theirs was a harsh reality: World War I had begun. In June 1914, in Sarajevo, Austrian crown prince Franz Ferdinand had been assassinated by a Serb nationalist, setting in motion an armed conflict between two European power blocs: the Central Powers of Germany and Austro-Hungary; and the Allies—Britain, France, and Russia. The two sides had a history of competition and mutual distrust. By September of that year, the German advance on Paris was stopped by the Allies at the Marne River, where for the next three years the two sides would battle in horrifying trench warfare along a three-hundred-mile front.

Created from Within

In his films for Keystone, Charlie Chaplin stands out distinctly from the other performers. In Chaplin: His Life and Art, *biographer David Robinson provides insight into the quality that not only made Chaplin films different from Keystone films but made Chaplin a tremendous, world-wide success.*

"Keystone comedy was created from without; anecdote and situations were *explained* in pantomime and gesture. Chaplin's comedy was created from within. What the audience saw in him was the expression of thoughts and feelings, and the comedy lay in the relation of those thoughts and feelings to the things that happened around him. The crucial point of Chaplin's comedy was not the comic occurrence itself, but Charlie's relationship and attitude to it. In the Keystone style, it was enough to bump into a tree to be funny. When Chaplin bumped into a tree, however, it was not the collision that was funny, but the fact that he raised his hat to the tree in a reflex gesture of apology. The essential difference between the Keystone style and Chaplin's comedy is that one depends on *exposition*, the other on *expression*. While the expository style may depend upon such codes as the Keystone mime, the expressive style is instantly and universally understood; that was the essential factor in Chaplin's almost instant and world-wide fame."

A Better Deal

Charlie's contract with Keystone was set to expire in mid-December 1914. He demanded a salary of $1,000 per week, a sum that would enable him to keep financing his films. Sennett balked, claiming that the amount demanded was more than he himself earned; Chaplin reminded his employer that people lined up outside movie theaters to see the Little Tramp, not Mack Sennett. During the negotiations, another movie company called Essanay (George K. Spoor and "Bronco Billy" Anderson: S and A) agreed to pay Chaplin $1,250 per week, much more than he was making at Keystone. When Keystone hesitated, Charlie signed with Essanay.

While proud of his financial triumph, and confident of his future in motion pictures, Chaplin felt uncomfortable about leaving Sennett and the crew and performers behind. In his autobiography he recalled the difficulty of separation: "It was a wrench leaving Keystone, for I had grown fond of Sennett and everyone there. I never said goodbye to anyone, I couldn't."[38]

Chapter

4 The Most Famous Man in the World

With more control over his Essanay films than he had had at Keystone, Chaplin found work as grueling at the Essanay Film Company in 1915 as it had been in Sennett's organization the year before. While he put out films less frequently now—roughly one every three weeks, instead of one a week—he worked just as hard planning and perfecting those films, the majority of them two-reelers. He made his first Essanay film at the company's Chicago studio, then did his next five at the company's studio in Niles, California, not far from San Francisco. From Niles, he went to Los Angeles, where he rented studio space and put out the rest of his films for Essanay.

Of course, he needed a troupe of players to work with. Bud Jamison, a large, baby-faced man, played the role of the oversized bully made famous by Mack Swain at Keystone. Leo White, lean and energetic, and with operetta experience, specialized in playing aristocrats in top hats and goatees. Most prominent of the comics Chaplin brought from Chicago was a balding man with an oval face and permanently crossed eyes: Ben Turpin also wore a toothbrush mustache and had a prominent Adam's apple. He didn't have to act funny—he just looked funny. And he was a very talented comedian. Chaplin

also found a leading lady, twenty-year-old Edna Purviance, a college girl from Lovelock, Nevada, with no acting experience. She was blonde and very beautiful, and Chaplin was captivated by her. They would have a secret romance. Purviance appeared with Chaplin in thirty-five films over the next eight years.

Cross-eyed comedian Ben Turpin was among Chaplin's talented troupe of performers at Essanay.

The Essanay Films

Chaplin had a busy year at Essanay. In his role as director, he scrambled to build on what he had picked up from his year at Keystone, becoming more proficient at editing and understanding how to highlight himself in the films. He also learned to frame his full figure for the majority of a film, to highlight his exceptional ability as a mime. At this time, he rarely used close-ups of facial expressions.

Most significantly, though, Chaplin accomplished two important things during his year at Essanay. He made great steps forward in terms of the development of the Little Tramp character, and he introduced social commentary into his work. All the while, his popularity grew.

The Developing Tramp

The development of the Tramp is especially evident in three 1915 films. In *The Champion* (March 1915), which features a boxing match with Charlie as the referee, we see a hint of a different dimension of the character. Chaplin appears for the first time caressing a flower. Some writers have connected this moment with the fact that Chaplin, in 1915, had romantic inclinations toward leading lady Edna Purviance. Fragments of love letters that Chaplin wrote at the time prove his deep feeling for her.

The Tramp (April 1915) expands on the romance theme as Charlie's pursuit of love ends in failure. We watch him save a farmer's daughter from hooligans and watch him win again, foiling the hooli-

gans' plot to rob the farm. Though in love with the farmer's daughter, he realizes he does not belong in her life when her young, handsome fiancé appears on the scene. As the film ends, we see the Tramp turn his back and walk away, dejected, toward the horizon—a moment of misfortune that makes him sympathetic to his audiences. But as the camera's iris closes, the little man livens his step, showing that he is unvanquished.

In *The Bank* (August 1915), Chaplin again pursues the theme of unrealized romance. Here he is a bank janitor who mistakenly believes that a beautiful teller (Edna Purviance) is in love with him. After discovering that the teller really is in love with the cashier, the dejected janitor falls asleep next to his bucket and mop and dreams of saving the teller from a robbery; she kisses him in gratitude. Then the janitor wakes up and the reality of his situation sets in: he is kissing not the teller but his mop, and, looking up, he sees the bank teller nearby, kissing the cashier. With this film, the Little Tramp had gone, in the words of author Roger Manvell, from "the burlesque villain who gets into countless scrapes and emerges from them with engaging ingenuity to the far more appealing 'down-and-out,' hanging onto odd jobs by the skin of his teeth, more victim than victor in most situations."[39]

Social Commentary

Chaplin's films for Essanay also contained social commentary. In *Work* (June 1915), Charlie and his boss are decorators in a rich man's house, which they succeed in demolishing by the film's end. Along the

Chaplin and on- and off-screen romantic interest Edna Purviance in Work, *a successful comedy that contains social commentary on poor working conditions.*

way, Chaplin shows the ugly side of work, most strikingly as a form of oppression, even slavery: at the opening of the film, harnessed to a wagon filled with hardware, he is made to pull first his boss, then another—and heavier—man. Though comedy prevails as Charlie struggles with the load, the message of poor working conditions, including heartless bosses, comes through. Audiences were sympathetic, and the film was successful: "It was such aspects of Chaplin's vision that found the hearts of the great mass audience of the early twentieth century."[40]

Police (May 1916) was probably Chaplin's first statement on hypocrisy, which he perceived as one of society's ills. The hypocrisy is exhibited by a pious reformer who robs a blind man, as Charlie, playing an ex-convict, looks on. Charlie's character goes on to join another criminal in an attempt at robbery, but their intended victim, played by Edna Purviance, moves Charlie with her kindness and makes him see the error of his ways.

Leaving Essanay

Near the end of his full year with Essanay, Chaplin considered renewing his contract with the company. In addition to his creative success, he had had a terrifically lucrative year. Indeed, midway through the year, having each new film more successful than its predecessor, he had asked for a change in his contract; Essanay complied, granting him a $10,000 bonus for each picture.

But even with this increase, Chaplin decided to let the marketplace decide his worth. Essanay tried to keep him, but the highest bidder for his services was the Mutual Film Corporation. Chaplin, aged twenty-six, concluded a deal with Mutual for $10,000 a week, with a signing bonus of $150,000. He made $670,000 in twelve months. A publicist writing for Mutual could gleefully boast, "Next to the war in Europe Chaplin is the most expensive item in contemporaneous history."[41]

Coming of Age

By paying Chaplin such a huge sum, Mutual was announcing that the movie industry had come of age in America. It was a business, like other businesses, and Chaplin's salary was justified because the revenues from the rentals of his films to distributors on a yearly basis would easily exceed it.

At this time, Hollywood moviemakers delighted in their importance and prosperity. Sid Grauman, a prominent businessman who owned Grauman's Chinese Theater, the finest cinema in town, promoted coming movies by sending jalopies with banners racing up and down the boulevards. He also required prominent actresses and actors to leave their footprints and handprints in wet cement in front of his establishment. Following the fabulous success of people like Mack Sennett and D. W. Griffith, fortunes were being made rapidly by filmmaking entrepreneurs. Salaries for film stars skyrocketed. Luminaries like screen stars Jean Harlow and Rudolph Valentino were highly visible, appearing at clubs and raging parties at night and in the gossip columns of the local newspapers the next morning.

In 1915 Americans preferred to distract themselves with movies while the war across the Atlantic raged on. At this time, most Americans believed it was not their country's responsibility to join a conflict between nations with a long history of warring. President Woodrow Wilson publicly refused to see any difference between the Central Powers and the Allies. In fact, Wilson was reelected in 1916 on the popular slogan, "He kept us out of war."

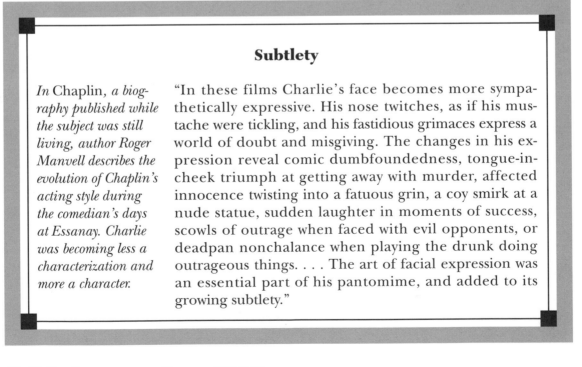

Subtlety

In Chaplin, *a biography published while the subject was still living, author Roger Manvell describes the evolution of Chaplin's acting style during the comedian's days at Essanay. Charlie was becoming less a characterization and more a character.*

"In these films Charlie's face becomes more sympathetically expressive. His nose twitches, as if his mustache were tickling, and his fastidious grimaces express a world of doubt and misgiving. The changes in his expression reveal comic dumbfoundedness, tongue-in-cheek triumph at getting away with murder, affected innocence twisting into a fatuous grin, a coy smirk at a nude statue, sudden laughter in moments of success, scowls of outrage when faced with evil opponents, or deadpan nonchalance when playing the drunk doing outrageous things. . . . The art of facial expression was an essential part of his pantomime, and added to its growing subtlety."

Chaplin (far left) with members of his Mutual stock company, including (from right to left) his brother Sydney, Albert Austin, Eric Campbell, press agent Carl Robinson, Henry Bergman, and John Jasper.

Mutual

Ready to begin fulfilling his contract with Mutual, Chaplin gathered a stock company (group of performers). He brought Leo White and Edna Purviance from Essanay. New players were lean and serious-looking Albert Austin, and giant Eric Campbell, "the ideal Goliath to his own David."[42] Dedicated and versatile Henry Bergman made his debut in *The Pawnshop* and remained a member of Chaplin's entourage for many years.

The Mutual films, which have been identified by one critic as "a series of comic essays on the trades and professions,"[43] are rich in inventiveness and often effective in the way they introduce pathos (human suffering) to arouse sympathy or pity in the audience. They also reveal Chaplin's continuing growth as a director. In his book *Classics of the Silent Screen*, Joe Franklin cites Chaplin's Mutual films as "a flawless welding of brilliant comedy and really moving [pity due to sympathy for a person, real or imaginary]."[44] Among the films he created for Mutual, *The Pawnshop, The Rink, Easy Street*, and *The Immigrant* are all considered classics.

The Pawnshop

In one of his most famous films, Charlie is employed in a pawnshop. He desperately tries to keep his job and win the hand of the owner's daughter (Edna Purviance). After quarreling with a coworker (Albert Austin), then ruining the merchandise of a customer (again, Albert Austin) in "one of the greatest scenes Chaplin ever made," he knocks out a crook (Eric Campbell) trying to rob the store's vault and becomes a hero, winning the girl.[45]

In *The Pawnshop*, Chaplin displays extraordinary comic creativity. His funnier gags include drying dishes and cups—and

The Pawnshop, one of Chaplin's most famous films, is filled with creative gags.

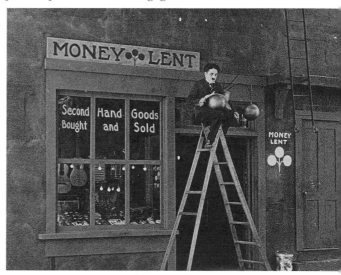

even his own hands—by passing them through a clothes wringer, and later reducing a bewildered customer's alarm clock to pieces. He also uses transposition—the identification of an object as if it were another—to create humor. An electric cord stretched across the floor becomes a tightrope. Doughnuts from the table of the pawnbroker's daughter become heavy dumb bells. Chaplin also makes comedy out of incongruity (the unexpected or inappropriate); for example, he takes his sandwiches out of a safe. One Chaplin biographer declared "Of all Chaplin's films *The Pawnshop* is the richest in gag invention."[46]

The Rink

In *The Rink*, Charlie is an inept waiter who lives another life as Sir Cecil Seltzer, a graceful skater at a local rink. At the rink, he saves a girl (Edna Purviance) from the advances of one of his restaurant customers, the influential, hot-tempered and hot-blooded Mr. Stout (Eric Campbell). The girl invites Charlie to her roller skating party, where he again meets up with Mr. Stout. The two men proceed to turn the party into a riot, from which Charlie

In The Rink, *Chaplin used a technique called undercranking to create the illusion that he is skating faster than life.*

escapes by hooking the rear bumper of a passing car with his cane and rolling off into the distance.

As director of *The Rink*, Chaplin used a technique known as undercranking to highlight his scenes on roller skates. The term comes from the days when film was cranked through the camera by hand—to undercrank, or crank too slowly, resulted in the acceleration of the movement of filmed images when they appeared on the screen. Seeing Chaplin skating faster than life makes him appear that much more graceful.

Easy Street

In *Easy Street*, Chaplin is a vagabond turned policeman who cleans up slummy Easy Street and its monstrous bully, played by Eric Campbell. Religion and romance have their parts in the film, too—Chaplin begins as a vagrant who is moved to change his life after meeting pretty missionary Edna Purviance during a meeting at the Hope Mission. At the end of the film, he escorts Purviance back to the mission for Sunday service.

Mime and author Dan Kamin points out that by the time of filming *Easy Street*, Chaplin had become quite adept at a number of skills, including finding "the best framing, angle, and distance from the camera to present his performance."[47] Kamin cites a scene from *Easy Street* in which Charlie sits on a chair without realizing it has no back—of course, he tumbles backward. But Chaplin knew the best camera angle for the gag: he shot from directly in front of the chair, so that his upper body disappeared as it fell backward.

Easy Street *starred Chaplin as the vagrant turned policeman, and Eric Campbell as the giant bully.*

Shot from another angle, the effect would not have been as surprising or humorous.

The Immigrant

The Immigrant, an especially funny and moving film, continued Chaplin's evolution of style in the sense that pathos was part of the performance. The story in the film as we know it is simple: Charlie and Edna are immigrants who meet on a ship bound for America. They are separated upon arrival, but accidentally meet again later in New York. Both down on their luck, they are discovered in a cafe by an artist who promises to hire them for modeling. Buoyed by the promise of security, the couple go off to get married.

One factor in Chaplin's success as a director was his willingness to experiment with a film until it worked for him. The original story line of *The Immigrant* had begun with a cafe scene, in which Henry

Bergman as the menacing waiter is demanding that Charlie, who cannot pay, settle the bill. After much shooting, two things occurred to Chaplin: first, Henry Bergman was not menacing enough, and he was replaced by Eric Campbell in the role of the waiter. Second, there had to be a reason for the cafe scene—and thinking about the characters, Chaplin came up with the idea of the ship of immigrants sailing to America.

Chaplinitis

The great Chaplin popularity explosion began in 1915. In that year, he was voted, month after month, the best male comedian by influential *Motion Picture Magazine*. Newspapers and magazines featured cartoons about him, and there were Chaplin dolls and Chaplin books. There were even songs about Charlie, like "That Charlie Chaplin Walk," "Those Charlie Chaplin Feet," and "Charlie Chaplin, the Funniest of Them All." In France, where he was called simply Charlot, there was a dance called the Charlot one-step.

Imitators quickly arrived on the scene. Especially successful was a comedian named Billie Ritchie, who dressed exactly like the Little Tramp and appropriated most of his facial expressions and other gestures. Ritchie, who had worked with Karno, came out with a blatant film impersonation on the heels of each Chaplin release. For example, Chaplin's *Work* was followed by Ritchie's *The Curse of Work*. Ritchie claimed that Chaplin had derived the Tramp character from a Ritchie character; Chaplin and critics dismissed Ritchie's claim.

Interestingly, Chaplin was not fully aware of the extent of his fame until early 1916. In February, he took a train east to join Sydney in New York, where they were seeking new offers for Charlie's services.

Chaplin's willingness to experiment as a director contributed to the ultimate success of The Immigrant, *a funny and moving film.*

Sydney now devoted all his time to his brother's business affairs. During the train trip, crowds gathered at railroad stations across the country, and there was a tremendous reception for Charlie in New York City.

Before age thirty, Charlie Chaplin had won tremendous popularity in America. There wasn't a soul who didn't know of the Little Tramp—even in prison. When his films were shown at the New Jersey State Prison at Christmastime in 1916, hardened convicts were reportedly beside themselves with laughter.

Chaplin's popularity continued into the following year. In March 1917, the film magazine *Photoplay* announced that managers of cinemas showing Chaplin films had to keep retightening the bolts that held down the theater seats—Chaplin's audiences had laughed so hard the seats came loose! Costume balls were the rage in 1917, and magazine writers reported that nine out of ten men attending one of these parties were dressed as the Little Tramp. Also in that year, a holdup man in a Cincinnati bank was disguised as the Little Tramp.

Comic Transposition

Chaplin often used comic transposition, or the comic identification of an object as another object. In The Pawnshop *(Mutual 1916), he examines an alarm clock brought in by a dejected customer, played by Albert Austin. Biographer David Robinson, in* Chaplin: His Life and Art, *explains the comedy that follows.*

"Charlie becomes a doctor and the clock his patient as he sounds it with a stethoscope and tests its reflexes. Suddenly it is a rare piece of porcelain as he deftly rings it with his finger tips. He drills it like a safe. He opens it up with a can-opener and then dubiously smells the contents with a look that declares them putrid. Momentarily the clock becomes a clock again as Charlie unscrews the mouthpiece of the telephone and transforms *that* into a jeweler's eye-glass. Having oiled the springs, he produces a pair of forceps and becomes a dentist as he ferociously pulls out the contents. Extracting the spring, he measures it off like a ribbon from nose to fingertip. He snips off lengths, then tips out the rest of the clock's contents onto the counter. When they start wriggling like a basket of worms he squirts them with oil. Having now demolished the alarm clock, he sweeps the contents back into the empty case and hands it back to the dazed Austin with a shake of the head and a look of grave distaste."

French posters advertise Chaplin's films. By 1917 Chaplin's Little Tramp was internationally recognized.

be out exercising in the sun. Another commentator accused him of being "a moral menace. His is the low type of humor that appeals only to the lowest type of intellect."[49]

Some voices warned ominously that Chaplin's great appeal might not last. In *Photoplay*, a writer asked:

> What is to become of Charlie Chaplin? Will the little genius of laughter slowly relegate himself to comic history, or will he, changing his medium of expression, pass to higher and more legitimate comedy? He must do one or the other: no one stands still on the highroad of artistic creation. Progress or retrogression is the universal lot, and Chaplin's cycle of dirt and acrobatics is about to run.[50]

Displeasure

Not everyone admired Chaplin's work, including some film critics. During his year with Essanay, he was cited for his "vulgar" comedy. Some took offense at one scene in *Work*, where Charlie slips a lampshade over a naked statuette, which he then wriggles, causing it to do a suggestive hula dance. Other films were criticized for tastelessness, even for obscenity. Said Fred Goodwins, a critic writing at that time: "His fame was at its zenith here in America when suddenly the critics made a dead set at him. . . . They roasted his work wholesale; called it crude, ungentlemanly and risqué, even indecent."[48]

Some commentators blamed Chaplin's films for causing athletic young men to stay inside dark theaters when they should

The Whole World Laughed

Chaplin's alleged "cycle" ran, all right, but not in the direction his detractors hoped for and predicted. The fact was that Chaplin, as one writer declared, had indeed made the whole world laugh. The silhouette of the Little Tramp was recognized internationally.

In Europe, populations uprooted by war perceived the Tramp's experience as their own, as did the immigrant populations of America. They, like him, were outsiders, regarded with suspicion. They, like him, counted on their pluck, their spirit, to pick themselves up after defeat and walk away, looking with determination for new opportunities.

Some basic qualities of the Little Tramp were understood the world over. In the prize fight featured in *The Champion*, Chaplin compensates for his small physique, as writer Frank Magill says, by "using his wits—and in this case a pet bulldog—to compensate for his lack of physical strength."[51] Audiences worldwide easily understood the drama of strong against weak, and they loved to see the weak triumph.

Finally, Chaplin had presented something unique. Besides his great talent, he demanded a new relationship with his vast audience. Even in *Kid Auto Races at Venice*, the first film in which he directed himself as the Little Tramp, he showed a fascination for the camera, and a need to be its focus of attention. Audiences had never before been confronted by such a character. And audiences responded. One writer summed up the Chaplin phenomenon of 1917:

In The Champion, *the Little Tramp uses his wits to compensate for his lack of physical strength.*

He is, I believe, the most widely known man in the world. They know him almost as well in Japan and Paraguay and Spain as we do here. Because of that he has attained an almost legendary significance in the eyes of millions of people; they give him something akin to the homage given to [stage actress Sarah] Bernhardt and Shakespeare and [champion boxer] John L. Sullivan. These millions could never have that feeling for a Senator, a diplomatist, a millionaire. But Charlie! "What is he like?" they say, breathlessly. "How does he walk and talk?"[52]

5 Challenges of Art and Life

In 1917 Charlie Chaplin appeared to have it all: he was young, he was fabulously wealthy, he was the most famous man in the world. His rags-to-riches success story rivaled any fiction produced by Hollywood writers. However, life cannot be expertly cut, edited, and finished as a work of film art, and in the years ahead Chaplin was to face unexpected challenges—personal, political, and creative—that threatened to undo him.

Loneliness

Lured by a million-dollar contract, on June 17, 1917, Chaplin signed with First National Exhibitors' Circuit. With First National he would have almost complete control over his work: the company only distributed and exhibited films—Chaplin himself would provide the finished product, created at his own studio, built on a five-acre lot in the Hollywood area.

All the money in the world, though, could not keep Chaplin from loneliness, his greatest affliction at this point in his career. His loneliness, he would always claim, was largely due to the shyness that had plagued him since childhood. In his autobiography he recalled one painful moment in New York at the height of his popularity.

My loneliness was frustrating because I had all the requisite means for making friends; I was young, rich and celebrated, yet I was wandering about New York alone and embarrassed. I remember meeting the beautiful Josie Collins, the English musical comedy star, who suddenly came upon me walking along Fifth Avenue. "Oh," she said sympathetically, "what are you doing all alone?" I felt I had been apprehended in some petty crime. I smiled and said that I was just on my way to have lunch with some friends; but I would like to have told her the truth—that I was lonely and would have loved to have taken her to lunch—only my shyness prevented it.[53]

His work consumed him at this time, and one casualty of his long hours was his relationship with Edna Purviance. The pair simply drifted apart, to their mutual regret, and Chaplin's loneliness increased.

But even when Chaplin was away from work and trying to relax, he found it hard to be comfortable around people—especially other actors and actresses. His autobiography contains these recollections:

Meeting the stars at various Hollywood parties, I have come away skeptical—maybe there were too many of us. The atmosphere was more challenging than friendly, and one ran many gauntlets to and from the buffet in vying for special attention. No, stars amongst stars gave little light—or warmth.[54]

There were, however, some stars who provided light for Chaplin. He cultivated relationships with cinema stars Douglas Fairbanks and Mary Pickford, as well as British writer H. G. Wells. There were friendships outside Hollywood, too: he and Sydney were close, as always. The brothers also made sure that their mother Hannah was taken care of in a hospital back in London. And in 1917 Charlie received a letter from Wheeler Dryden, the half-brother he hadn't seen since childhood. In time Sydney, Charlie, and Wheeler were happily reunited, and Wheeler found a permanent place on Charlie's staff.

Backlash

Despite his popularity, Chaplin faced public backlash, first because of his enormous and well-publicized salary. Chaplin tried to ignore the public's expressions of envy and bitterness. He claimed that the money he earned was of little importance, saying that he was simply glad to be financially secure, hence able to spend as much money as necessary to produce his films. The money had given him an enormous freedom, he stated to the press. "It means that I am left free to be just as funny as I dare, to do the best work that is in me and to spend my energies on the thing that the people want. I have felt for a long time that this would be my big year and this contract gives me my opportunity. There is inspiration in it. I am like an author with a big publisher to give him circulation."[55]

The public had another gripe with Chaplin: his stance on World War I. A

(Left to right) Douglas Fairbanks, Mary Pickford, Chaplin, and D. W. Griffith. Chaplin's loneliness after his breakup with Edna Purviance was eased in part by his friendship with Fairbanks and Pickford.

Chaplin speaks to a huge Wall Street crowd in 1918 during his tour promoting the sale of Liberty Bonds. Unable to serve as a soldier, Chaplin used the tour as an opportunity to support the U.S. war effort.

British citizen, Chaplin had chosen not to leave the United States to fight for his native country. Subsequently, British audiences had mixed feelings about Chaplin. They loved his films but disapproved of his nonparticipation in the war effort. Representatives of the British government had told him he was more valuable as an entertainer than as an infantryman, but to many Britons, such statements were a poor excuse for Chaplin's failure to join them physically as well as in spirit.

Until early 1917, Americans knew about Chaplin's stance toward the hostilities in Europe but remained ambivalent; this attitude changed, though, when the United States entered the war in April 1917 after the Germans sank three American merchant ships. Then, in what seemed like a pent-up rush of emotion, came a shower of letters expressing disappointment, anger, and even hostility toward Chaplin and his nonfighting status. Some letter writers even threatened his life.

The outpouring of negative sentiment upset Chaplin. He claimed he wanted to be a man of the world—not of any particular nation. Yet he wanted America—and the world—to know that even though he believed he could do more for the war ef-

fort by making entertaining films, he was indeed willing to fight for his country. Less than two months after signing with First National, Chaplin declared, on August 4, 1917, "I am ready and willing to answer the call of my country."[56] In a show of willingness, less than two months after signing with First National, Chaplin appeared at a recruiting office in the United States, where he was told he was underweight and not fit to be a soldier. And in the spring of the following year, he left Hollywood for Washington on a tour promoting the sale of Liberty Bonds, which were special financial instruments purchased by citizens to help support the war effort. In any event, it was Britain that had the authority to call him to duty, and the British Embassy made it clear that Britain's compulsory draft law was not in effect in the United States.

Chaplin's War Effort

While agreeing to more speaking engagements, Chaplin continued to believe that he could best assist the war effort by doing what he did best: making films. After fin-

Chaplin's contract with First National gave him almost complete control over his work. The popular A Dog's Life *was Chaplin's first film for the company.*

film. Released on October 20, 1918, it revealed his feelings about war. Charlie plays a recent inductee, incompetent as a soldier, who appears first in a uniform decorated with, among other things, a mousetrap, eggbeaters, and a cheese grater. When handouts of food arrive, Charlie receives a chunk of cheese so foul that he dons a gas mask. The food is useful only as a kind of grenade to be thrown across the battlefield and into the German trenches.

Charlie dreams of battlefield heroics. With the idea of infiltrating the German command disguised as a tree, he knocks out enemy soldiers with his branches, but runs into trouble when one soldier tries to cut him down for firewood. He eventually succeeds in knocking out the Kaiser (the German emperor). But Charlie's battlefield success is only a dream—he wakes up, finding himself still the raw recruit, the odd man out.

The film was received with much critical enthusiasm. One critic called it "a bravely jolly little picture, excellently

ishing the well-received *A Dog's Life*, his first film for First National, he made *The Bond* for the Liberty Loan Committee. This film, distributed for viewing in the fall of 1918, was meant to encourage people to buy war bonds. Chaplin played a few scenes in the short film, focusing on the important bonds of love, marriage, and friendship, as well as the most important bond of all, the Liberty Bond.

Shoulder Arms

Chaplin's second film for First National, *Shoulder Arms*, was no mere propaganda

Shoulder Arms, which reveals Chaplin's feelings about war, was well received by audiences and critics.

done, and a concentration of brilliancies, in a comedy way, like the light-shooting facets of a diamond."[57] American and European audiences welcomed the comedy, too. The timing for the release of this parody of war was superb—audiences saw it at the time the Armistice was signed—on November 11, 1918—ending the global conflict. People were more comfortable laughing, now that the time of violence had come to an end.

Regarding the end of the war, Chaplin would say:

> Living without a war was like being suddenly released from prison. . . . The Allies had won—whatever that meant. But they were not sure that they had won the peace. One thing was sure, that civilization as we had known it would never be the same—

that era had gone. Gone, too, were its so-called basic decencies—but, then, decency had never been prodigious in any era.[58]

The signing of the Treaty of Versailles on June 28, 1919, formalized the German defeat. Dead on both sides totaled 8.4 million.

United Artists

As the war ended, Chaplin was looking into the future of his career in films. He, Pickford, and Fairbanks talked about their desire to produce and distribute their work independently. Spurring their concern was talk of a possible merger among the motion-picture studios that would

One Critic's Opinion

Film critic and talk-show host Joe Franklin was a great admirer of Chaplin, though he claims that Chaplin's films changed for the worse when Chaplin joined First National in 1919. Says Franklin in Classics of the Silent Screen:

"After *Shoulder Arms,* something happened. The critics had been noting, and praising, the deeper meaning in some of Charlie's films, and in their enthusiasm for subtleties and symbolism they went overboard, often reading into the film philosophic content that Chaplin had hardly intended. But Chaplin was impressed, and changed the format of his films. They were still comedies, but the pace slowed, the laughs were fewer and more obvious, and the pathos and drama were stepped up. The remainder of his films for First National— *The Pilgrim, The Kid, The Idle Class, Sunnyside,* and others, all with glorious moments, were, as a whole, a distinct retrogression from the great Mutuals and the first two at First National."

Chaplin signs the papers for the creation of United Artists in 1919, along with co-founders Griffith, Pickford, and Fairbanks. Chaplin's contract with First National prevented him from making pictures with United Artists until 1923.

result in a monopoly. Actors learned that the company executives, now all working together, could cut down on the terrifically high salaries that motion-picture giants commanded.

On January 15, 1919, Chaplin, Fairbanks, Pickford, and D. W. Griffith announced the creation of United Artists, a film distribution company. This announcement inspired the anonymous comment: "The inmates have taken over the asylum."[59] However, because of his contract with First National, Charlie would not be able to make films for United Artists until 1923.

Distraction

In 1920 Chaplin looked for a new film project; as usual he gained inspiration by observation. He reported in his autobiography having seen four-year-old Jackie

Coogan appearing on stage with his father, an eccentric dancer. Young Coogan displayed a few dance steps himself, and that sent Charlie's mind spinning with ideas. He began work on a film in the fall of 1919 and continued into the new year.

During the filming of his new picture, Chaplin was distracted by the media attention surrounding his break-up with his first wife, Mildred Harris. The couple had been married in private in 1918, but the marriage had soured following the death of their three-day old son. Late in 1919, the couple had agreed to get a divorce. "We separated in a friendly way," Chaplin would later recall, "agreeing that she was to get the divorce on grounds of mental cruelty, and that we would say nothing about it to the press."[60] But the press found out, and the stories of their unhappy marriage, often cruelly exaggerated, and their divorce proceedings, often messy, appeared in the press throughout the year.

The Kid

Though distracted, Chaplin finally finished his film, and in February 1921 First National released *The Kid*. It was the first feature-length film written and directed by Chaplin. *The Kid*, at six reels, was ninety minutes long. It was also an immediate success. *Theater Magazine* praised it as "a screen masterpiece."[61]

The Kid tells the story of a tramp who raises an abandoned baby boy. The comedy comes mostly out of situation rather than out of incident—and the situation is, of course, Charlie, with no experience as a

Hailed as "a screen masterpiece," The Kid was the first feature-length film written and directed by Chaplin.

parent, trying to attend to the needs of a baby. He feeds the baby by putting a nipple on the spout of an old coffee pot, and a potty is created by placing a chair with a hole cut in the seat over a cuspidor (a receptacle for spitting, to accommodate users of snuff and chewing tobacco). The gags continue, and when the boy is five Chaplin is still struggling to be a decent parent.

Although he had been warned by other directors that a film should be either comedy or tragedy, Chaplin was able to add pathos to comedy and meet with great success. One film historian explains: "Chaplin's ability to shift between comic and tragic modes is encapsulated in a sequence [in *The Kid*] in which the police try to take the boy away. The Tramp foils their efforts in slapstick fashion, but when he and the boy share an emotional embrace as they are reunited, the effect is all the more heartrending because of the comic context."[62]

After *The Kid*, Chaplin turned out three short films: *The Idle Class*, with Charlie playing both the Tramp and a drunken husband; *Pay Day*, which "even made the ushers laugh in the theatre"[63]; and *The Pilgrim*, in which he plays an escaped convict turned cleric. *The Pilgrim* featured Edna Purviance in her last role as Chaplin's leading lady.

Pleased with public and critical reception to his efforts, Chaplin also attained some measure of satisfaction later in 1921 by bringing his mother to the United States. Hannah had been living in a private hospital in London for years, sustained financially by checks from Charlie and Sydney. In California, she was set up in a bungalow by the sea and lived there for several years, certainly a great beneficiary of Charlie's hard-fought success.

Sobbing?

Chaplin showed his comic genius in The Idle Class *(1921). In* Magill's Survey of Cinema: Silent Films, *editor Frank Magill supplies the commentary.*

"Chaplin plays two characters, The Tramp and an alcoholic millionaire. The confusion of identities is conventionally amusing but Chaplin demonstrates his mastery of the medium by the staging of one of his most clever gags. The millionaire has been spurned by his wife. His back is to the camera, and he appears to be sobbing with increased agitation, but when he turns around viewers see that he has been vigorously mixing a drink in a cocktail shaker and that his expression is unemotional. The combined qualities of silence and the camera's close proximity to the trembling figure creates the illusion which Chaplin so adroitly exploits for comic effect."

Having now fulfilled his contractual obligations to First National, Chaplin joined United Artists and made plans for his new feature-length movie. He would never make another one of his celebrated short films.

The Twenties

In the decade after World War I, America tried alternately to return to normal and to accommodate change. The Republican administrations that held office during the Twenties pledged conservativism and a return to traditional American values; at the same time, Americans were drinking, dancing, and generally rebelling against established norms and standards of behavior in this time period, which would be known as the Jazz Age.

In the arts, it was a time of flowering creativity and experimentation. Theater, music, dance, and drama produced exceptional new talents, including the composer-songwriter team of George and Ira Gershwin, dancer-choreographer Martha Graham, and playwright Eugene O'Neill. In literature, F. Scott Fitzgerald wrote stories about the rich who lived, loved, and drank in splendor on the shores of Long Island, while, as Gerald Mast points out, the "readers who devoured Fitzgerald's stories about the wild lives of the very rich were themselves solidly bourgeois, middle class."[64]

A Woman of Paris

A Woman of Paris, Chaplin's first film for United Artists, was released in October 1923. It is not a comedy. The story tells of star-crossed rural lovers who, turned out by their parents, decide to run off together to live in Paris. Tragedy follows from the lovers' failed relationship—one dies and the other, in penance, vows to care for orphaned children.

Critics asked why the king of comedy would want to abandon the genre that had brought him unprecedented success. One reason was that Chaplin wanted to create a role for Edna Purviance, with whom he had worked for many years. Though only in her late twenties, Purviance no longer had the very youthful qualities audiences of the time expected in a leading lady. Still, Chaplin felt obliged to her, remained good friends with her, and was concerned about her personal finances—and wanted to help her by giving her the lead role in the film. He was also impressed with the work of the German director Ernst Lubitsch, who focused on psychological dramas, in which performers revealed their psychology by subtle action.

Critics came down harshly on the film. Many insisted that Chaplin's taste was old-fashioned, his approach melodramatic and heavy-handed. Too much theatricalism, they insisted. He defended himself against this charge:

> To me theatricalism means dramatic embellishment . . . the abrupt closing of a book; the lighting of a cigarette; the effects offstage, a pistol shot, a cry, a fall, a crash; an effective entrance, an effective exit—all of which may seem cheap and obvious, but if treated sensitively and with discretion, they are the poetry of theatre.[65]

Edna Purviance did not receive good reviews for her performance. Her career faltered, but Chaplin, devoted and sentimental, kept her on contract for the rest of her life, though she was no longer cast in his films. She would later appear as an

Chaplin directs a scene in A Woman of Paris, *his first dramatic film. Critics called the film melodramatic and too theatrical.*

extra in *Monsier Verdoux* and in *Limelight*. She died in 1958.

The Gold Rush

Chaplin was faced with creating a story for his next film. In his search for ideas, he looked at photographs of Alaska, the Klondike, and the gold prospectors who headed there in the Twenties; at around the same time, he stumbled on the story of the Donner Party, a group of eighty-seven pioneers from Illinois who set out for San Francisco during the winter of 1846–47. They ended up lost in the Sierra Nevadas, however, and half the group perished. Those who were rescued had survived by resorting to cannibalism.

Chaplin's new film, *The Gold Rush* (August 1925), represented a monumental effort. Production began in the snow-covered mountains of Nevada in the spring of 1924 and lasted fourteen months. Costs for the film soared to over a million dollars.

The story featured the elements of pathos and comedy that were emblematic of Chaplin's greatest films. Lost and alone in a snowstorm, Charlie finds refuge in an abandoned cabin. The cabin's owner appears—Black Larsen, a villain—and soon the two men are joined by a third, Big Jim. After a fight, Black Larsen is subdued and sent out into the storm, but he kills two mounted police who follow him and makes off with their sled. Meanwhile Big Jim, delirious from hunger, goes after Charlie, who appears to him as a huge chicken. They part friends, and Big Jim next meets up with Black Larsen, who has stolen Jim's gold claim. Big Jim is knocked unconscious; Larsen dies in an avalanche.

Chaplin on location in the Nevada mountains during the shooting of The Gold Rush, *a huge production that cost over a million dollars to make.*

Meanwhile, Charlie goes to town and falls in love with a dance hall girl, played by Georgia Hale, who uses the vagabond Charlie to keep a handsome suitor off balance. As a joke, she agrees to come on New Year's Eve with the other girls to the cabin Charlie is watching for a fellow prospector. Charlie cooks an elaborate dinner, but Georgia and the girls never show, and Charlie falls asleep. In a dream, he is the life of the party and performs the famous "dance of the dinner rolls," which features Charlie, seated, delightfully manipulating two dinner rolls stuck into two forks on the table before him; his own "huge" head and the tiny roll "feet" appear to belong to the same body. Then he wakes, alone. He wanders down to the barroom and watches on the periphery as Georgia is embraced by the handsome

Inspired by the story of the Donner Party, The Gold Rush *was the film that Chaplin wanted to be remembered by.*

man. Then she remembers her date with Charlie, but it's too late.

Big Jim reappears, his memory clouded from a blow delivered by Larsen, and joins up with Charlie to search for the lost claim. The two return to Larsen's cabin, which nearly blows off the mountain's edge in a windstorm, and discover the document. As the movie winds down, Charlie and Big Jim are millionaires on a ship headed back to civilization. Charlie finds Georgia tucked away in the ship's hold, and they are happily united.

Critics praised the film. The *New York Times* reported that "it is the outstanding gem of all Chaplin's pictures, as it has more thought and originality than even such masterpieces as *The Kid* and *Shoulder Arms*."[66] The critic for the *New York Herald*

Tribune gave the film an enthusiastic review, then added that "Praising one of Mr. Chaplin's pictures is like saying that Shakespeare was a good writer."[67] Chaplin biographer Roger Manvell later wrote: "Like all Charlie's stories, *The Gold Rush* is a fable, each episode an enrichment of the underlying situation—poverty and hunger for men in dire straits and the basic human need for companionship and love."[68]

Chaplin himself admired the film, saying that this was the one he wanted to be remembered by. He would surely not, however, want to be remembered by the scandal that followed in the wake of *The Gold Rush.*

Suffering Through Scandal

While meeting with success on the screen, Chaplin's life off-screen again took an unhappy turn. He had married his second wife, sixteen-year-old actress Lita Grey, in November 1924. Soon after the marriage Charles Spencer Chaplin Jr. was born, and then Sidney Chaplin, named after Charlie's brother. Both sons would enter the acting profession.

Despite the joy they had experienced upon the birth of their children, the couple broke up in December 1926, and Lita Grey filed for divorce in January 1927. Like his first marriage, Chaplin's second marital calamity played out before the public. The divorce proceedings were especially trying. Lita Chaplin brought scandalous charges against her former husband, accusing him of abusive treatment toward her and involvement in affairs with other women. The court barred Chaplin from removing any of his assets, including his films, from the state of California. Additionally, at this time the government claimed that he owed approximately $1.1 million in unpaid taxes.

The press had a field day. They splashed Chaplin's picture across their pages and printed any dirt that was available, from any source. The nation read with curiosity and shock the descriptions of Chaplin's behavior toward his wife. Film stars had been identified with lurid off-screen behavior since the beginning of the decade, when comedian Fatty Arbuckle had been forced to retire from the screen because of his part in the death of a woman due to sexual excesses at a wild Hollywood party. Now, editorials calling for a ban on Chaplin films met with support from outraged citizens, and some states responded.

All this took its toll on Chaplin. Seeking to escape the commotion, he fled to New York in 1927, thereby halting shooting of *The Circus*, his work in progress. In New York, depressed and exhausted, Chaplin suffered a nervous breakdown. He was confined to a bed for a period of time. He feared that his career was over and that he would lose his vast fortune.

Some matters, however, were resolved. The divorce was granted in August 1927. Lita Chaplin accepted as settlement about a million dollars and the custody of the two boys. Chaplin paid his back taxes to the government. Then he returned to work on *The Circus*. As evidence of the pain caused by this period of his life, Chaplin gave his second marriage and divorce only one brief paragraph in his autobiography and never mentioned Lita Grey's name.

Chaplin's second wife, Lita Grey, with their sons Sidney and Charles Jr. Amidst scandalous accusations by Grey, the couple divorced after only two years of marriage.

At about this time, Chaplin suffered another loss: on August 28, 1928, Hannah Chaplin died in California. Charlie had seen her the day before her death, at Glendale Hospital, where she was being treated for an infected gall bladder. Mother and son had been able to laugh together. The next day, Chaplin was at the studio working when he got the news. He rushed to the hospital to view the body, and later wrote movingly of his feelings:

> You could see that she suffered no more . . . I suppose when life tortures, death is very welcome. She was still in the hospital on a bed. I had seen her the day before and she was in agony. But then the following day, suddenly

seeing somebody beloved and small, you think of all the events of life. . . . It's really moving . . . I couldn't . . . I couldn't touch her. No, I couldn't touch her.[69]

The Circus

The Circus appeared in January 1928. Chaplin himself was surprised, years later, to find that he actually liked the film—while he was making it, he had been preoccupied and miserable. Indeed, biographer Roger Manvell notes: "*The Circus*

The Circus was filmed following the breakup of Chaplin's marriage and the death of his mother. Despite the unhappy circumstances under which it was made, the film was a success.

leaves the impression of melancholy and loneliness rather than of humor."[70]

The plot is simple. After having a hilarious encounter with a pickpocket and then the police, who believe the innocent tramp to be a criminal, Charlie seeks refuge in a circus, where his adventures with the pursuing police and a vicious donkey leave the audiences in stitches. He falls in love with a bareback rider (Merna Kennedy), who is also the circus master's daughter, and unwittingly becomes the star of the show. His romantic aspirations are sunk when the bareback rider falls for the new tightrope walker, Rex. Charlie knows that Rex is better suited to protect the girl than he is. At the end of the film, the circus wagons pull out, leaving Charlie sitting alone in the spot where he had once been a performer. He gets up and walks off, away from the camera, twirling his cane and hopping now and again, showing spirit and indomitable will.

Predictably, audiences loved his new film, and critics applauded it. One New York critic reported that "the hardest-boiled crowd in town went to the midnight opening on Friday and laughed off all its mascara."[71]

The Challenge of Sound

With the opening on Broadway in October 1927 of *The Jazz Singer*, sound made its debut in American films; within a year, sound had become standard fare in movie houses across the country. Audiences became accustomed to hearing characters talk—even at the expense of action on the screen. In its infancy, movie sound was so striking that audiences didn't really notice

Al Jolson in The Jazz Singer, *the first motion picture with a synchronized soundtrack, or "talkie."*

the poor dramatic quality of the first "talkies."

Though comfortable with his silent films, Chaplin felt the ever-increasing pressure to put out a film with dialogue. He certainly did not want to do a talking film just to show off the sound of it. He decided to stay with what he did best, and in 1931 he released *City Lights*. The film is not a "talkie," but it is not entirely silent: a soundtrack takes over for the human voices, and real sound effects accent some comic sequences.

City Lights

City Lights tells of the love of a tramp for a blind flower girl—and how his own sacrifices make it possible to raise the money for surgery that restores her sight. Chaplin said that he got the idea for the film from the story of a clown who lost his sight in an accident and is told by his doctor to hide his blindness from his sickly daughter, who might go into shock if she knew the truth. In the original story, the clown, pretending he has vision, keeps bumping into things—which makes his daughter laugh with delight. For his film, Chaplin made many changes in the story, including the decision to have the flower girl blind instead of the clown.

With *City Lights*, Chaplin presented the character of the Tramp in its full, final form:

> As time passed and he imbued the character with more and more of himself, the Tramp became at the same time both universal and unique; universal in his representation of the dreams and longings which are shared by all, and unique in those characteristics which gave Chaplin his particular genius.[72]

The film contains one of the most moving scenes in film—at the very end, the flower girl first gazes on the tramp

The wildly popular City Lights *featured Virginia Cherrill as the blind flower girl, and Chaplin as the tramp who makes her dreams come true.*

who has made her dream come true. It is an extended moment in which the camera, close-up, explores the deep emotions of the tramp, played by Chaplin, and the girl, played by Virginia Cherrill, as with sight restored, she slowly recognizes her benefactor by the touch of her hand on his. "The whole scene lasted seventy sec-

onds," Chaplin later recalled, "but it took five days of retaking to get it right."[73]

City Lights has often been cited as Chaplin's greatest film. His brand of pantomime stood out in great contrast to other films of the day, which put too much emphasis on talk for talk's sake. Said one writer, "Critics and public alike took time out to consider whether sound really had added so much to the movies after all, when the best film of the year was a silent!"[74]

While critics found *City Lights* delightful and picked up on the work's blend of comedy and social comment, audiences turned out in droves to see the film, first in Los Angeles, where Chaplin attended the world premiere, and later across the nation. On the morning of the New York premiere, Chaplin met a publicity man who was exuberant with the report of long lines already forming. Chaplin then appeared at the theater in time for the first show:

> I saw half an hour of it, standing with the crowds at the back of the theatre, in the midst of happy intensity relieved continuously by sudden outbursts of laughter. That was enough. I came away satisfied and gave vent to my feelings by walking all over New York for four hours. At intervals I passed the theatre and saw the long unbroken line that went round the block.[75]

6 Social Issues

The decade of the Thirties is usually clocked beginning with the Wall Street Crash of late 1929. Over the course of several days in October 1929, for several reasons, including the nation's high rate of unemployment, the stock market collapsed, collapsing with it many fortunes made during the prosperity of the Jazz Age. Conservative investments of middle-class Americans who believed that prosperity would never end collapsed as well.

Collapsed, as well, were the carefree social attitudes of Americans; in the Great Depression that followed—a time of severe economic slowdown in America and throughout much of the world—the party was clearly over. Simply struggling through a period of sudden or continued unemployment and general hard times was now the sole concern of most Americans.

Chaplin himself was untouched by the great drop in stock market prices. In 1928 he had read a book on economics that convinced him that the present high unemployment in the United States would cause a financial disaster. Showing the financial acumen that served him all his life, he decided that the stock market at that time was an unsafe place to have one's money. He sold all his shares at high prices and lost nothing when prices tumbled.

It wasn't simply the Crash that had put so many Americans out of work; many were unemployed because they had been replaced by machines. In an era of increasing modernization, many intellectuals and artists in the Twenties and Thirties saw the dehumanization of man. They saw factories taking control of people's working lives. They saw the machine supplanting the worker as the object of respect among the captains of industry.

Chaplin saw all this, too. Looking for an idea for his next film, he began to dwell on a story passed on by a young newspaper reporter. "Hearing that I was visiting Detroit, he had told me of the factory-belt system there—a harrowing story of big industry luring healthy young men off the farms who, after four or five years at the belt system, became nervous wrecks."[76]

Modern Times

Five years after the release of *City Lights*, Chaplin addressed the industrial assembly line system in *Modern Times* (1936), which was a love story at its core but touched on many current themes, as well. For this film, Chaplin introduced Paulette Goddard.

Chaplin with his third wife, actress Paulette Goddard. The couple fell in love during the making of Modern Times.

hair from platinum blonde to black, and announced that she would be his new leading lady. Romance between them blossomed as Chaplin, twice divorced and more than twice Goddard's age, was charmed by the young actress. The two became inseparable, and they married just as *Modern Times* was released.

The film begins with the title, "Modern Times is the story of industry, of individual enterprise—humanity crusading in the pursuit of happiness." The story is about a mild factory worker—the Little Tramp—whose assembly line job causes him to go mad. He winds up in a hospital, a jail, and a department store, fighting to survive in an increasingly hostile world with a gamine (young girl who roams the streets of a city) by his side. The two end up in a cheap cabaret, where she dances and he's a singing waiter—the only time Chaplin's voice is heard on the soundtrack. The film ends with the Tramp and the gamine walking arm-in-arm toward the mountains—where future struggles surely await.

When she met Chaplin in 1932, Goddard, then twenty-one, had already played in feature films and a few comedy shorts directed by Hal Roach. Chaplin bought her contract from Roach, changed her

Modern Times, *which featured the last screen appearance of the Little Tramp, received mixed reviews and was misunderstood by many audiences.*

How He Worked

In his book Chaplin, *Roger Manvell paints a portrait of Chaplin at work, quoting the recollections of Chaplin's son, Charles Jr.*

"When Charlie worked, everyone observed his need for uninterrupted concentration, culminating in the actual making of the films. The family was sacrificed ruthlessly. 'Everyone associated with him during these periods, either in the studio or at home, was drained.' He worked for prolonged periods on his scripts—more than two years, says Charles [junior], on *Modern Times*, beginning immediately on his return from his tour overseas. He loved the act of writing, but hated any interruption while doing so. There he sat, head bent, glasses on nose, a 'tender, absorbed expression on his face.' When he was happy, he would sing; when he was depressed, he would keep quiet. The moody spells were oppressive, familiar to everyone who was close to him. Relaxation meant a game of tennis, a real release, something which others might find in alcohol."

The critical response to *Modern Times* was mixed. The film was banned in Germany and Italy for containing "communist statements" and was not widely distributed in the United States for the same reason. The film had some success in the United States, as well as in the European countries that viewed it, but seemed to have little effect on audiences in the Soviet Union.

Audiences had trouble with the film. For instance, since the Tramp and the gamine routinely stole to eat, some believed the director was condoning stealing to relieve hunger. Mostly, though, American audiences did not understand Chaplin's satire on the advent of machines, and they questioned the wisdom of making a silent film eight years after talkies had

come on the scene. In America, the movie failed to make a profit.

Innocence Lost

Modern Times was the last screen appearance of the Little Tramp. In Chaplin's next film, about a madman on a mission to drive the world to war, there were signs of the Tramp. But as one writer notes, "then the image faded and disappeared. Only the old films remained, but in them the Little Tramp would always live. He would be skating on the rink, eating the watermelon, examining the alarm clock, dining on his shoe, dancing with the nymphs, rescuing Edna [Purviance], and walking down the lonesome road as long as film endured."[77]

Mocking Hitler

Chaplin had known about a real madman for years. During the Thirties, as Adolf Hitler became increasingly prominent, the physical resemblance between Chaplin's Little Tramp and the German fascist was widely observed; among Chaplin's crowd, it was the subject of amusement. "He stole my makeup!" Chaplin often complained, to the delight of his friends. Later, as Chaplin had suspected, with Hitler's rise to power in 1933 and his subsequent racist speeches and actions, the Nazi leader had become a serious threat to world peace.

In 1938 Chaplin began writing the script for a movie that would mock Hitler. The film would utilize sound—the role of Hitler would be a speaking part. As Hitler, Chaplin could exploit his own talent for faking foreign languages, as he had done with a nonsense song near the end of *Modern Times*. On the other hand, as a Jewish barber, Chaplin would concentrate mainly on communicating through pantomime, speaking only when necessary.

As Chaplin's new film went into production in 1939, the world watched Hitler's Germany continue its assault on Europe. Having annexed Austria and part of Czechoslovakia in 1938, Germany went on to occupy the remainder of Czechoslovakia in 1939. In August, Hitler signed a nonaggression pact with the Soviet Union, effectively eliminating the Russians from interfering with his plans. When Germany invaded Poland on September 1, 1939,

World War II was ignited. Two days later, Britain and France declared war on Germany. By the following summer, Hitler and his chief ally, Italian dictator Benito Mussolini, were unchallenged on the Continent.

At the outbreak of war, Chaplin postponed work on the film. It was a tense time. In addition to events of global significance, Chaplin had lately received anonymous letters threatening disruptions of the new film, and even riots at theaters. After a few days, though, he resumed shooting, deciding, in the words of author Roger Manvell, that "ridicule was after all as good a way to expose the pretensions of Hitler as serious drama."[78] The film was released in the early spring of 1940.

In 1939 Chaplin began production on a movie intended to mock German dictator Adolf Hitler (pictured). Riots and threats prompted postponement of the film's release.

While The Great Dictator *was not without controversy, many critics admired Chaplin for his bravery in mocking the Nazi leader.*

The Great Dictator

The Great Dictator, which costars Chaplin's new wife Paulette Goddard, takes place in the imaginary country of Tomania two decades after a military defeat. Chaplin plays a Jewish barber who was a soldier in the war but now has amnesia; the barber and Hannah (Goddard), his new friend from the ghetto, struggle against the goons and political bullies of the country's leader, Adenoid Hynkel—also played by Chaplin. The barber and the dictator are look-alikes.

While seeking a loan from a rich Jewish banker, Hynkel stops his attacks against the Jews of the ghetto. When he is turned down for the loan, however, Hynkel resumes and steps up his aggression. Hannah flees the country, and the Jewish barber fights valiantly but winds up in a concentration camp. He escapes, however, and the scene switches to Hynkel, who is planning an invasion of neighboring Austerlich. To avoid any mis-

understandings, though, he must make clear his intentions to his rival, Benzino Napaloni, dictator of Bacteria (played by Jack Oakie). While trying to intimidate, it is Hynkel himself who is intimidated by the brash Bacterian leader during a raucous meeting. Finally, Hynkel and Napaloni reach an understanding.

Hynkel decides to do some duck hunting, with the idea that the people of Austerlich will not suspect that Tomania is preparing to launch an invasion. But the boat capsizes, and Hynkel swims to shore, where, thought to be the escaped Jewish barber, he is arrested. The Jewish barber himself is then mistaken for Hynkel and is taken to make a radio broadcast on the eve of the invasion of Austerlich.

The Great Dictator ends with a six-minute speech, given by the Jewish barber. The barber begins by declaring to the world that people really want to help one another and that humankind has somehow lost its way: "We think too much and feel too little"; then the plea goes out to Hynkel's soldiers to lay down their arms, to not "give yourselves to these brutes—who despise you—enslave you—who regiment your lives—tell you what to do—what to think and what to feel!" By the end, the barber has shared his vision of a new world, where the clouds lift and the sun shines down: "We are coming into a new world—a kindlier world, where men will rise above their greed, their hate and their brutality."[79]

The long closing speech was extremely controversial. It was not that audiences disagreed with the sentiments. Rather, they found the speech to be overblown and out of character; they found it unnatural, and so did critics. Said one film historian: "The overt didacticism [obviously instructional nature] of the film's final speech, a fervent and sincere but overlong and sentimental appeal for world peace, is a dramatic letdown."[80]

Critics weren't let down by the film. They generally admired Chaplin's audacity in mocking the German strongman. One reviewer had an especially interesting insight into Chaplin's achievement in this film:

Charles Chaplin is the only artist who holds the secret weapon of mortal laughter. Not the laugh of superficial gibing that self-complacently underrates the enemy and ignores the danger, but rather the profound laughter of the sage who despises physical violence, even the threat of death, because behind it he has discovered the spiritual weakness, stupidity and falseness of his antagonist.[81]

Social Consciousness

Biographer Roger Manvell contends that by the mid-1930s Chaplin had developed a sense of social consciousness, which appeared fully formed in the 1936 film Modern Times.

"It moves in the direction of social comment, social satire. Technically, it remained in effect a silent film, except for the ironic gibberish Charlie sang at the end. But its conception derived from the increasing social conscience which Charlie had been developing from his wide reading, his discussions with men and women involved in politics and social studies, and from his travels and intuitive, emotional response to the society at his time—this was the period of the world depression, of industrial rehabilitation and expansion, and the era of Lenin, Stalin, and the Russian revolution, and of Hitler and the oppression of Europe. *Modern Times* was the first of Charlie's films, whatever his intentions, to lay itself open in certain sequences to wild, nonsensical charges of being 'Leftist' propaganda."

Audiences didn't appear to be let down, either. British audiences, in the thick of war, completely enjoyed *The Great Dictator*, reveling in its gags and in the actual resemblance between Chaplin and Hitler. In America, still at peace, audiences tended to be reserved. One young viewer said "I liked the picture because it was down to earth and it shows the suffering of the people in Europe and it shows Charlie Chaplin's true character."[82]

The film was a success. It premiered in New York and went on for a fifteen-week run. It broke records in London. It turned out to be the highest grossing film yet for Chaplin, who was nominated for both best actor and writer of the best original screenplay for the Academy Awards of 1940. Jack Oakie, as Napaloni, was nominated for best supporting actor, and the picture was nominated for best picture.

But Chaplin found the press to have become increasingly hostile. One reason was that he had not previewed the film in Hollywood, much to the chagrin of the press there, who felt ignored. He would later explain that he had too much riding on the film to risk a poor Hollywood review. He also spoke with conviction in support for the Soviet Union in their battle against Hitler. Invited to give speeches at rallies for organizations like the American Committee for Russian War Relief, Chaplin, appreciative of the sacrifices that Russians made fighting against Nazi Germany, graciously accepted. It was no surprise that the film was banned in Italy, and later in France when the Vichy government, which collaborated with the Germans, was established.

In retrospect, Chaplin expressed doubt about the film. "Had I known of the actual horrors of the German concentration camps, I would not have made *The Great Dictator*. I could not have made fun of the homicidal insanity of the Nazis. However, I was determined to ridicule their mystic bilge about a pure-blooded race: As though such a thing ever existed outside of the Australian Aborigines!"[83]

In the wake of the success of *The Great Dictator*, there was sadness for Chaplin. He and Paulette Goddard were breaking up. During the filming, Chaplin had subjected his third wife to much hard criticism, sometimes driving her to tears. After the film's official opening, she left him for good. She would finalize her divorce in Mexico in 1942.

More Scandal

After the breakup of his marriage to Goddard, Chaplin found himself caught in another scandal with another young actress. Joan Barry had come to his studio for a screen test in June 1941 and was put under contract. Chaplin found her attractive, describing her as "a big handsome woman of twenty-two."[84]

But as he saw more of her, he found something disturbing about her behavior, marked by sudden appearances and exits, which seemed symptomatic of an unbalanced mind. She would come to see him well after midnight, sometimes drunk, sometimes breaking windows in his house when she was not admitted. Eventually he announced to her that their relationship was over. But she kept intruding in his life, and he could not escape her. He started keeping a gun in his bedroom. The press found out about the ongoing drama and focused public attention on it.

Actress Joan Barry brought about a paternity suit alleging that Chaplin was the father of her daughter.

Two years after their first meeting, Barry broke into Chaplin's house, was arrested and put into detention, and claimed she was pregnant with Chaplin's child. A paternity suit followed. Chaplin, insisting on his innocence, refused to settle out of court. He demanded justice and was willing to brave the publicity that would come from a court battle.

At this time, he met the woman with whom he would spend the rest of his life. Oona O'Neill was the eighteen-year-old daughter of playwright Eugene O'Neill. A professional actress, she was intelligent, understanding, and accommodating. Chaplin later recalled being moved by her "luminous beauty, with a sequestered charm and a gentleness that was most appealing."[85]

Oona and Charlie married secretly in 1943, at about the time of the filing of the Barry paternity suit. When the press found out about the marriage, they exploited the difference in ages of Chaplin and his new bride. When Joan Barry heard the news, she broke down in tears. The public was quick to condemn Chaplin, seen now as the ruin of not one but two young women's lives. Chaplin remembers: "The newspapers were black with headlines. I was pilloried, excoriated and vilified [very severely criticized]."[86]

In 1944 the federal government got involved, claiming that Chaplin had violated

In 1943 Chaplin married Oona O'Neill, the eighteen-year-old daughter of playwright Eugene O'Neill. Chaplin was criticized for marrying a woman so many years his junior.

the Mann Act, prohibiting transporting an underage girl across state lines for sexual purposes. The official basis for this charge was that back in 1942, Chaplin had paid Barry's train fare to New York and she had used his money again for the trip back to California. The charges, as writer Roger Manvell remarks, "were ludicrous."[87]

Apparently, however, some people in authority wanted to punish Chaplin for his politics: his public support for the Soviet Union, America's sudden ally after the country joined the war against Hitler in 1941. Even with America's commitment to fight alongside the Soviet Union, most Americans were wary of the Soviets and their communist government.

Thus with the paternity suit awaiting trial, Chaplin was indicted on charges of having violated the Mann Act. Joan Barry was the first witness. She testified, with great emotion, that Chaplin had indeed transported her across state lines for the purpose of having intimate relations. Chaplin was the last witness, and he denied all accusations, insisting that intimate relations between him and Barry had ended well before her trip to New York.

The jury believed Chaplin. He was found not guilty on all counts. That night, he dined quietly with Oona, who was four months pregnant. "We wanted no newspapers, no telephone calls. I did not want to see or speak to anyone. I felt empty, hurt and denuded of character."[88]

More hurt followed. Chaplin still had the paternity suit to deal with. In the trial, which began in December, the jury, obviously influenced by Joseph Scott, the cunning and fiery attorney for the plaintiff, could not reach a verdict. At the April 1945 retrial—with Scott again arguing Barry's case—the jury found Chaplin guilty. Outraged, Chaplin requested another retrial, but the court, after four weeks of contemplation, denied his mo-

---

Citizen of the World

While many in the United States and Great Britain denounced Chaplin for his lack of patriotism, Chaplin defended himself in his autobiography, citing what had been done in history for the sake of patriotism.

"The fact is I am no patriot—not for moral or intellectual reasons alone, but because I have no feeling for it. How can one tolerate patriotism when six million Jews were murdered in its name? Some might say that was in Germany; nevertheless, these murderous cells lie dormant in every nation. . . . Naturally, if the country in which I lived were to be invaded, like most of us, I believe I would be capable of an act of supreme sacrifice. But I am incapable of a fervent love of homeland, for it has only to turn Nazi and I would leave it without compunction."

The screenplay for Monsieur Verdoux *was nominated for an Oscar in 1947. However, its controversial content caused many theater owners to boycott the film.*

tion. Exhausted by the drawn-out sequence of legal events, and knowing that the damage to his reputation could never be undone, Chaplin was nonetheless relieved that the whole affair was behind him. In 1946 he returned to moviemaking.

Monsieur Verdoux

Chaplin's next film, *Monsieur Verdoux* (1947), seemed to be an exercise in cynicism and a response to his recent experiences as defendant in the Barry paternity suit. In this film, Chaplin played a cold-blooded murderer of wealthy spinsters who justifies his actions by citing the overwhelming brutality of war, big business, and politics against the individual. His crimes, claims the murderer, are nothing compared to those committed by "civilized society."

Chaplin was very pleased with the film, which took him only twelve weeks to produce. In his autobiography, he wrote proudly: "I believe *Monsieur Verdoux* is the cleverest and most brilliant film I have yet made."[89] The screenplay for the film was nominated for an Oscar in 1947.

Censors did not think highly of the film, though. The Motion Picture Association had the power to demand changes or cuts in Hollywood films, or ban them outright, and the Chaplin film was cited for offensive passages, particularly those expressing Verdoux's views toward his crimes. Chaplin communicated with Joseph Breen, the official in charge of censorship, and was able to convince him to allow the film to be shown. Even then, though, some cities banned the film.

Critics and audiences noted the difficulty of this work. Many found fault with Chaplin for using such a repugnant character as the protagonist—Verdoux was cer-

Anti-Semites

Charlie was accused by anti-Semitic elements in America and Nazi Germany of being a Jew. In Chaplin: His Life and Art, *Chaplin's friend Ivor Montagu mentions it.*

"Charlie is not a Jew or of Jewish origin. He attributes his black curly hair in youth to a Spanish strain. But he had rigorously refused ever to deny publicly that he is a Jew. He says that anyone who denies this in respect to himself plays in the hands of the anti-Semites. From Germany in the thirties I sent him the filthy Nazi propaganda book of photographic portraits of Jews, *Juden sehen dich an.* His portrait was included and the caption began . . .'This little Jewish tumbler, as disgusting as he is boring . . .' I like to think it had some part in stimulating *The Great Dictator.*"

tainly no Little Tramp. Some critics, though, commented on the higher purposes of the film, pointing out that here Chaplin spoke for the individual who battled the forces of a hostile government. Other critics emphasized that Chaplin was showing us a man who had lost his sense of morality because of a sense that the world had lost its sense of morality. As one writer declared, Chaplin "was actually trying to make the point that mankind must avoid future wars."[90]

The film ran for a short time in New York, and appeared across the country for only three weeks after its initial release on April 11, 1947. In October Chaplin pulled it from distribution while planning a new promotional campaign. However, several conservative political organizations, including the Legion of Decency, deemed *Monsieur Verdoux* full of communist overtones, and more theater owners boycotted the film. Two years later, Chaplin stopped the distribution of the controversial film altogether.

In 1947 a new crew joined the ranks of those eager to attack Chaplin and his films: members of a congressional committee that came to be known as HUAC—House Un-American Activities Committee—arrived in Hollywood and began summoning people in show business who were suspected of knowing or being Communists. While Chaplin kept busy planning his next film, HUAC was busy making plans for him.

7 Banishment and Return

Created by Congress in 1938, the House Un-American Activities Committee had gained notoriety in the years after World War II as competition between the Soviet Union and the United States rose and relations between the former allies deteriorated. The committee focused its efforts on hunting for Communists and other people in American society thought to be guilty of treason as demonstrated by their attitudes toward the Soviet Union. In the course of its work, the committee used questionable evidence and improper tactics to make some people it had targeted look like Communist Party members or sympathizers. As a result, many people's careers were ruined, and some of the most prominent victims were in show business.

Although Chaplin never had an opportunity to defend himself against the charges in an official context, HUAC publicly claimed that he was "un-American." He had, for example, associations with such well-known leftists as the composer Hanns Eisler and the painter Pablo Picasso. HUAC member John T. Rankin of Mississippi demanded in a June 1947 debate in Congress that Chaplin be deported: "He has refused to become an American citizen. His very life in Hollywood is detrimental to the moral fabric of America. [By deporting Chaplin] his

loathsome pictures can be kept from before the eyes of the American youth."[91]

In defending himself, Chaplin would often say simply that he was not a Communist. "Neither have I joined any political party or organization in my life," he would readily add.[92] Moreover, Chaplin stated time and again that he was willing to ad-

Chaplin talks to members of the press, defending himself against charges by the House Un-American Activities Committee that he was a Communist.

The Non-Conformist

In America, Chaplin was considered a Communist by some groups. In this passage from his autobiography, Chaplin defends himself with characteristic moral outrage and aggressiveness.

"Friends have asked how I came to engender this American antagonism. My prodigious sin was, and still is, being a non-conformist. Although I am not a Communist I refused to fall in line by hating them. This, of course, has offended many, including the American Legion. I am not opposed to that organization in its true constructive sense. . . . But when the legionnaires go beyond their legitimate rights, and under the guise of patriotism use their power to encroach upon others, they commit an offence against the fundamental structure of the American Government. Such super-patriots could be the cells to turn America into a fascist state."

dress his official accusers in public. But he never had the chance. Some commentators suggest that no one in the government wanted to risk putting Chaplin "on stage." Cagy HUAC members realized that if the great clown were given an opportunity to defend himself before a national audience, he could make the congressmen look like fools. Chaplin himself confirmed that in this respect, at least, the committee had been correct: "I'd have turned up in my tramp outfit—baggy pants, bowler hat and cane—and when I was questioned I'd have used all sorts of comic business to make a laughing stock of the inquisitors."[93]

Chaplin's popularity in America was now at a low point; yet a performance before HUAC would have drawn more laughter from his public than the recent *Monsieur Verdoux*.

Besides taking offense at the cynicism of his latest film, the controversy over his political leanings, and past scandals, Americans began to feel that Chaplin didn't really care about America, anyway. Why, after living in the United States for more than thirty years, had he not become a citizen? Chaplin's claim to be a "citizen of the world" no longer seemed a satisfactory reason.

Limelight

In 1951, Chaplin, now sixty-two, went to work on *Limelight*, which would be his last film in the United States. Indeed, it seemed the fitting finale to a life's work. He would say in his autobiography that the idea for the film came to him while watching a once-popular British comedian lose his hold on the audience during a performance. Chaplin wondered what had brought about this change.

Chaplin and Claire Bloom in Limelight, *a film that features Chaplin as an aging, alcoholic vaudeville comedian who has lost his popularity with his once admiring audiences.*

Limelight provides one possible answer. The protagonist, the old vaudevillian Calvero, once one of the most popular music hall comedians in England, has lost his touch with audiences because of old age, too much dignity, and a tendency to introspection. He also has become a heavy drinker.

Calvero meets Terry (Claire Bloom), a young, out-of-work dancer who thinks she has lost the use of her legs. With Calvero's encouragement, Terry summons the strength to resume dancing and seek employment. Calvero himself loses his nerve after an unsuccessful performance at a second-rate music hall, and the roles are reversed—now Terry, who feels strongly for the old man, consoles him. Terry lands a role and becomes a star, and Calvero, though having great affection for her, sees her falling in love with a young composer

(Charlie's son Sidney Chaplin), and realizes that this is best for the dancer.

Withdrawing from Terry's life, Calvero becomes a street musician, but eventually, Terry finds out and organizes a benefit show for him. Calvero and another older comedian, played by Buster Keaton, put on a wonderful comic performance. The audience applauds them heartily, and Calvero's belief in himself is reaffirmed. But Calvero is too old and frail for this kind of excitement, and his heart gives out. Unaware of the severity of Calvero's condition, Terry takes the stage to dance, and Calvero dies.

Like many other Chaplin films, *Limelight* contains autobiographical references. Some critics have pointed to the parallels between Calvero, dependent on alcohol, and Chaplin's father. Also, Terry's mother, seen slaving away at her sewing machine, determined to eke out a living for herself and her two children, is reminiscent of the young Hannah Chaplin.

There are many comic moments in *Limelight*. The most satisfying comic sequence is the performance of Chaplin and Keaton as the two old vaudevillians. Keaton had been a comedy star of the cinema in the Twenties, and some critics believed that his films, marked by subtlety and brilliant comic inventiveness, were superior to Chaplin's. Despite his initial success, though, Keaton never achieved the popularity enjoyed by Chaplin. Rather, he lived more or less in obscurity, and Chaplin was happy to bring him back to the public as a comic violinist.

While some critics found the film a bit too sentimental in places, *Limelight* earned wholehearted praise from others. One writer called it "a near-perfect work of art in the tradition of the swan song."[94] Another praised its quality of longing, which "whispers through the music; it passes across Chaplin's face in an emotional spectrum of variations; it creeps into the ballets and the tramp comedy routines, and it flows from the screen in the bittersweet contact between the audience and the drama."[95]

Deciding that *Limelight* should premier in London, the city of Calvero's triumph, Chaplin booked passage on the ocean liner *Queen Elizabeth*. There was excitement in the air as the Chaplins prepared for Oona's first trip to Europe. They had decided to take the children and spend six months on the Continent after promoting the film in London. There was something else in the air, though. Not long before leaving California, Chaplin told Oona and their friend Tim Durant that he had a feeling that he would not return.

Despite critical success in the Twenties, comedian Buster Keaton never attained the popularity enjoyed by Chaplin. The two great comedians appeared together in Limelight.

Banishment

On September 19, 1952, two days after the *Queen Elizabeth* set sail, Chaplin heard remarkable news over the radio. The U.S. attorney general had stated that Chaplin's reentry permit was being withheld. If he wished to return to the United States, he would have to appear before an Immigration Board of Inquiry, "to answer charges of a political nature and of moral turpitude."[96] It was announced that this action was being taken in accordance with a law prohibiting entry into the United States by people who advocated communism or associated with communist organizations. Both the attorney general and the FBI were investigating the charges against Chaplin.

When the ship docked at Southampton, England, Chaplin's first response to the press was philosophical. He insisted that he had no political convictions, and he acknowledged that the U.S. government could not be expected to go back on its word. He added that he would return to America to fight the charges raised against him. "All I want to do," he added, "is create a few more films. It might amuse people. I hope so."[97] His mild response to the news of his possible exile made perfect sense; he knew he was cut off from his assets in the United States, and he certainly intended to get them. He did, in fact, think he would return.

But it soon became clear that this political storm would not quickly pass. The Truman administration stood firmly behind its charges, and the American press was having a field day. Despite some media support, many writers and commentators agreed with the government's action. Nationally syndicated columnist Hedda Hopper, never a friend of Chaplin's, wrote "I abhor what he stands for. . . . Good riddance to bad rubbish."[98] At the same time, conservative groups like the American Legion picketed movie theaters showing *Limelight,* in many cases forcing the withdrawal of the film.

"Thank You!"

In Chaplin: His Life and Art, *writer Sidney Skolsky recalled the audience's response to Chaplin's "thank you" after the very first preview of* Limelight.

"A woman in the audience shouted, 'No! No! Thank you,' and then others in the audience took these words and shouted them to Chaplin. . . . Somehow I think this is the key to *Limelight*. It doesn't matter whether some people think it is great. The degree doesn't matter. This is not an ordinary film made by an ordinary man. This is a great hunk of celluloid history and emotion, and I think everybody who is genuinely interested in the movies will say, 'Thank you.'"

By November, Chaplin knew that a return to the United States was out of the question, and he acted quickly to recover his assets. Oona returned to Hollywood, hoping to get to the family possessions before the government did. Fortunately, she succeeded, and all the Chaplins' money was removed from the United States without interference. Chaplin's house, his studio, and his interest in United Artists would be sold off within two years. The Chaplins decided to settle in Switzerland—mostly because of the security of the Swiss banks.

Personally, Chaplin was disgusted. After all he had done to bring joy to Americans and to add to America's positive image in the rest of the world, this was the thanks he got. The following April he formally handed back his U.S. reentry permit, with this statement:

> I have been the object of lies and vicious propaganda by powerful reactionary groups who by their influence and by aid of America's yellow [sensation-oriented] press, have created an unhealthy atmosphere in which liberal minded individuals can be singled out and persecuted. Under these conditions I find it virtually impossible to continue my motion picture work, and I have therefore given up my residence in the United States.[99]

Sentiment in the United States against Chaplin lingered. A few community libraries showing his films were shut down by angry citizens. Negative articles still appeared in the press. Hollywood Boulevard's "Walk of Fame," opened in the late Fifties, with golden sidewalk stars representing the giants of the cinema, still did not admit a star for Chaplin: local property owners had angrily demanded its omission.

Life in Switzerland

Chaplin bought Manoir de Ban, a thirty-seven-acre estate near the city of Vevey, Switzerland, on Lake Geneva. The Chaplins adjusted well to their new country, and family life gave the aging entertainer much pleasure. It was clear to everyone that his life had changed infinitely for the better when Oona had entered it. He would say "I love my wife and she loves me. That is why we are so happy. . . . If you don't demand too much from each other—that, I think, comes nearest to being a formula

The Chaplins upon their arrival in Europe in 1952. The family settled in Switzerland and would eventually include eight children.

for happiness in marriage. The rest takes care of itself through tolerance."[100]

He extended this tolerance to his children, who included Geraldine, Michael, Josephine, Victoria, Eugene, Jane, Annette, and Christopher. Oona bore him eight, the last one arriving when Chaplin was in his seventies. He would always say that they made him happy.

And Oona was happy with him: "Charlie is a half-and-half personality. One half is difficult—the other easy. But I find we manage very happily. He is an attentive husband and a wonderful father."[101]

More Projects

Content with his life in Vevey, Chaplin was still eager to get on with his next project. In 1956 he directed his next-to-last film, *A King in New York*. Produced in England, the film was Chaplin's comment on the aggressive hunt for Communists by the government back in America, fired by Wisconsin senator Joseph McCarthy, who sought Communists in the motion-picture industry, as well as in the worlds of literature, music, sports, and politics.

The movie is about a king (Chaplin) who is displaced by a revolution in his small country and forced to make a living in New York. He comes to America believing that it is a country of ideals and hope, but quickly becomes disillusioned. Assisted by a young girl who has a job in television advertising, he is hired to make TV commercials promoting various products—including alcohol—but is repelled by each one.

The king takes in a boy named Rupert, whose parents have been called before a government committee investigating political affiliations. Suspect because of his protection of the boy, the former king is asked to appear before the committee which, after being doused with a firehose in a raucous courtroom scene, finds the defendant innocent of any wrongdoing. Rupert, however, with the thought of helping his parents, gives the committee

Many critics found A King in New York *disappointing, lamenting that Chaplin's pantomime ability had diminished.*

names of the parents' friends. Chaplin's character decides to leave New York and settle in Europe.

While some critics applauded the movie, most found no comparison between it and the standards set by such films as *City Lights* and *The Gold Rush.* Most critics observed that Chaplin was now an old man and that his pantomime was "but a glimmer of his once great gift."[102]

My Autobiography

Age may have diminished his pantomime skills, but it did not seem to affect his great ability to remember: in 1964 Chaplin published *My Autobiography.* Besides being the story of his life, the book tells the story of the times—the Twenties, the Great Depression, World War II, and the cold war. *My Autobiography* provides great insight into the growth of the motion-picture industry, too. One writer commented, "If one had only one book to read to understand a century of cinema, I would recommend *My Autobiography.*"[103]

The book opens with the eloquence and sentiment of a Dickens novel. Show-ing his fine skill as a writer, Chaplin recalls details from his bleak childhood in London. Indeed, he vividly brings to life the sad stories of his mother and father, his youthful entry into show business, the years with Karno, and his introduction to films with Mack Sennett at Keystone.

But then the book changes. Beginning with his year at Mutual, he often talks—and sometimes gossips—about the social life success had brought him, and speaks less of his films. Reading *My Autobiography,* one gets the idea that Chaplin began life swallowing up details of his experience, but ended by being swallowed by the very success he had worked so hard to achieve.

A Countess from Hong Kong

Two years after publishing *My Autobiography,* Chaplin made his final film. *A Countess from Hong Kong* is a comedy about an American millionaire (Marlon Brando) who keeps a beautiful stowaway (Sophia Loren) in his cabin as a luxury liner takes him back to America. The comedy is provided by the millionaire's efforts to keep the girl hidden.

Chaplin with his daughter Geraldine and Marlon Brando on the set of his final film, A Countess from Hong Kong.

Except for the cast and the fact that Chaplin directed it, *A Countess from Hong Kong* probably would have been ignored in the year of its release. This sentimental, often charming film was a misfit in the year that produced *Bonnie and Clyde* and *The Dirty Dozen.*

In 1966 Chaplin began work on a dramatic comedy called *The Freak,* which was to be the story of a girl who wakes up one morning to find she has sprouted wings. He worked on the project, begun at age seventy-seven, for the rest of his life; the filming was never completed.

Return

By the beginning of the 1970s, Chaplin began looking for new ways to make use of his films. With the help of a canny businessman, Chaplin began rereleasing them, primarily in America. He composed new musical scores for *The Circus, The Kid,* and *The Idle Class,* and the films received much praise from critics and the public.

Time had softened America's attitude toward Charlie Chaplin. By the 1970s, America, in the throes of self-criticism over its involvement in the Vietnam War, found tame the "subversive" statements made by Chaplin decades before. Moreover, a new, permissive generation enthusiastically discovered Chaplin through rerelease of his films. Generally, over the decades, interest in Chaplin's politics had receded while his contributions to film had come into focus.

In 1972 Chaplin was invited back to America. The details of the revocation of his reentry permit twenty years earlier had been long forgotten. The Academy of Motion Picture Arts and Sciences wanted to present him with an honorary Oscar. At age eighty-two, Chaplin was not sure he wanted to visit the country that had turned against him two decades before. According to an associate, he was persuaded to go by the opportunity to inspect a new camera that might help him speed up work on *The Freak*.

Two weeks before his eighty-third birthday, on April 2, 1972, Chaplin was greeted warmly at New York's Kennedy Airport. More than a hundred newspeople waited for him. Celebrities attended parties given in his honor. On April 5 he attended a gala reception and showing of his films at New York's Lincoln Center, where he received a three-minute standing ovation.

From New York, Charlie and Oona flew to Los Angeles, where he was to receive his honorary Oscar during the annual Academy Awards ceremony on April 10. On the flight, though, Chaplin became apprehensive. Candice Bergen, on assignment from *Life* magazine, recorded the moment: "He grew more and more nervous, sure he shouldn't have come. He looked fearful and trapped but made a brave attempt to fight it. 'Oh well,' he sighed, 'it wasn't so bad. After all, I met Oona there.'"[104]

Final years

During the last five years of his life, Chaplin tried to be as active as possible. He attended award ceremonies in his honor throughout Europe, and he was knighted by the queen of England. He began a new book—with the focus on his films—which he hoped would supplement his autobiography. He even created a new score for his

Chaplin's final years were quiet ones, spent with his wife and companion, Oona, by his side.

first film for United Artists, *A Woman of Paris*. He seemed determined to work until the end.

The last years of his life were spent quietly, and Oona was a great source of comfort to him. The couple would be driven by their chauffeur to the Swiss countryside, spend an hour or two in a quiet spot, then be picked up and driven home. When Charlie grew too frail to venture outdoors, Oona would sit for hours with him, holding his hand in silence. Death came peacefully to Charlie Chaplin in the early morning hours of December 25, 1977. He died in his sleep on Christmas Day.

The Importance of Charlie Chaplin

The world mourned the loss of Charlie Chaplin. The great surviving film directors were among the first to pay tribute. Federico Fellini called Chaplin "a sort of Adam, from whom we are all descended . . . there were two aspects of his personality: the vagabond, but also the solitary aristocrat, the prophet, the priest and the poet."[105] François Truffaut noted the importance of family to Chaplin: "He made beautiful films and beautiful children. Long and happy life to Geraldine, Josephine, Victoria, Jane and the others, and also all of our thanks and affection to Oona who made Charles Chaplin happy in his old age."[106]

The funeral was a quiet one, as he had asked for. It was held in Vevey on December 27, 1977, for family members. Chaplin's body was set in a coffin and covered with a silver and black cloak, then buried in Vevey Cemetery. Thus the great man, so active in life, was laid to rest.

Chaplin died in 1977 at the age of eighty-eight. He was laid to rest during a small, quiet ceremony at Vevey Cemetery in Switzerland.

Chaplin's coffin was robbed from his grave by kidnappers who demanded a large ransom for his body. Luckily, the coffin was recovered with Chaplin's body intact.

Grave Robbers

But not for long. On March 2, 1978, Chaplin's cemetery plot was visited by grave robbers. There was speculation in newspapers all over the world on who had taken the body and why. One popular contention pointed the finger at a neo-Nazi group, supposedly taking revenge for *The Great Dictator*. Soon, though, the real reason was revealed: kidnappers were holding the body for a ransom of 600,000 Swiss francs.

Oona refused to give in to the demands for money. She was taking the determined stance suggested by Charlie years before, when the couple had discussed what to do in the event that one of them were to fall victim to kidnappers. At first, she would tell the press only that her husband was "in heaven and in my heart."[107]

But when the kidnappers started making threats against her children, Oona knew she must seek help in dealing with the criminals. Fortunately, however, the kidnappers proved to be rather inept. After several weeks, the police were able to capture them as they arrived in an open field to pick up the money. The body was found in its coffin, buried in a cornfield about twenty miles from Vevey. The conspirators were later tried and convicted.

As horrible as the ordeal was for the Chaplin family, Charlie himself might have gotten a laugh out of the episode. And if not a laugh, then perhaps the plot for a new film. It was the kind of bizarre story that had always inspired his imagination.

The Importance of Charlie Chaplin

Charlie Chaplin was arguably the greatest comic genius of all time. By the time he signed with Mack Sennett and the Keystone Film Company in late 1913, Chaplin was already a seasoned performer, having won the hearts of audiences in music halls on two continents. But the talent he brought to the motion picture screen was unprecedented. No one in the short life of the Hollywood film industry possessed such blinding comic talent.

Chief among his comedic skills was his art as a mime. As Chaplin critics Raoul Sobel and David Francis contend, mime was Chaplin's "supreme gift. No amount of intelligence, perception, emotion and ideas could have taken its place, for without the ability to translate them into gesture and movement, 'the Little Fellow' would have remained a dead letter; a character Chaplin might have dreamed about but never have realized."[108] Mime masters like Marcel Marceau, Harpo Marx, and Red Skelton all freely acknowledged their debt to Chaplin's work.

Chaplin also showed range and evolution as a comedian. Early on, he sought to explore societal problems and the turmoil of the human heart through his comedy, which he fused effectively with pathos. Where people laughed at the Sennet films, they laughed and cried watching

Chaplin as the Little Tramp in one of his best-loved films, City Lights. *Chaplin's Little Tramp struck a responsive and sympathetic chord in audiences around the world.*

Chaplin's Little Tramp. The Tramp became a feeling person who demanded that audiences sympathize with him; he reached out, insisting on a bond between himself and the masses in the theaters. Indeed, Chaplin, through his Little Tramp, became famous for "the remarkable blend

Universality

Chaplin's films were seen and appreciated by audiences all over the world. The Oxford Companion to Film *offers a strong reason for his unbounded popularity.*

"His enormous popularity sprang from the universality of his appeal. Class barriers were transcended by his appearance, which could be seen as reduced gentility or ambitious poverty; cultural differences by the classical simplicity of his plots; and the normal bias in favor of the underdog was satisfied, in his earlier work, by his invariable triumph over bullying, rich, or glamorous adversaries while never changing his seedy appearance."

Struggles with Life

Because of his difficult childhood, Chaplin was always aware of life's struggles. In one of the final paragraphs of his famous autobiography, Chaplin discusses his perspective on life.

"I realize that time and circumstances have favored me. I have been cosseted [pampered] in the world's affections, loved and hated. Yes, the world has given me its best and little of its worst. Whatever were my ill vicissitudes, I believe that fortune and ill-fortune drift upon one haphazardly as clouds. Knowing this, I am never too shocked at the bad things that happen and am agreeably surprised at the good. I have no design for living, no philosophy—whether sage or fool, we must all struggle with life. I vacillate with inconsistencies; at times small things will annoy me and catastrophes will leave me indifferent."

of humor and pathos, poetry and slapstick that touches a responsive chord in audiences who recognize a humanity upon which the character is based."[109]

Charlie Chaplin was also the first "mass man" in American history, "the very first national and international craze generated by the motion picture industry."[110] He became available, through his films, to the people of America, who approved of what they saw and in turn created a market for more Chaplin films. And he obliged. Artifacts connected with him—statuettes, keychains, and other novelty items—were mass-produced and sold around the world. No one's silhouette was as widely recognized, no one's physical mannerisms were as lovingly mimicked.

One view is that Chaplin's Little Tramp was like any other product that people needed, and as a useful product it was greedily consumed: "Like those cre-ations of Edison, the Wrights, and Ford, his character added a new concept to help the evolution of mankind. Chaplin's new product entertained people; they did not question its mechanism, just as people everywhere were learning to consume without questioning."[111]

If the Little Tramp was a product, what did it provide for the consumer? Look at Chaplin's initial audience: the masses of working-class people, facing an increasingly mechanized society, including the horrors of the new machines of war that meted out death on the fields of Europe during World War I. The people needed distraction, they needed entertainment—and they needed to see themselves portrayed on the screen as simple and good, but challenged by a more and more demanding society. They needed, as Jean Boden contends, "a simple character facing the complexity of the industrial world."[112]

The Essence of Humanity

"In the movie world his silent outcry is part of each of us. He has become as indispensable to us as Mozart, Bach, Michelangelo and Da Vinci. . . . For a long time we shall see him running in front of mirrors which reproduce him infinitely in *The Circus* . . . we shall laugh at his gags in front of the statue in *City Lights* . . . we shall hold our breath before his boxing scenes . . . we shall be astonished to see him running away from cops with such grace and dexterity . . . we shall watch in wonderment as he changes himself into a lamp when pursued by cops tracking him down. No one in our lifetime will ever forget Chaplin's last look at the flower girl in *City Lights.* His eyes and tragic smile embrace all humanity and raise in our heart deep compassion. Chaplin remains a mythic poet, an angel, a seeing brother, a mime character representing the essence of humanity."

That simple character, of course, was the Little Tramp.

Finally, Chaplin was an outspoken individualist. He was a moralist who did not back down when the truth, as he saw it, needed to be told. While his attacks on society's hypocrisy and corruption appeared intermittently in his short films, it was in his feature-length films that he found his satirizing voice. Many artists might prefer to remain quiet about their convictions, to avoid the possibility of losing public support, even making enemies. This was not Chaplin's preference—especially when monsters like Hitler appeared on the world stage.

Before Chaplin, the burgeoning motion-picture industry ran as a system that subordinated a performer's individuality to the demands of the film corporations. But Chaplin, through his talent and outspoken individualism, set a valuable precedent: he was one of the first "stars" who fought for creative independence and won. And he remained fiercely independent: "Chaplin produced and owned his own pictures, ran his own studio, and released through United Artists; the success and popularity of his films guaranteed him theaters in which to exhibit them and profits to make more pictures just as he wanted to make them."[113] He became the symbolic father of the cinema by doing it all: writing, acting, directing, producing, owning, and even composing the music for his own motion pictures.

In a familiar scene from many of Chaplin's films, the Little Tramp walks off into the sunset. While the man is gone, his work remains, ensuring that the great comedian will not soon be forgotten.

Will His Work Survive?

Chaplin's great contributions to film and to world culture during the early years of the twentieth century—specifically the years 1914 to 1918—almost ensure that he will go down in history as a great artist of a certain time period. Roger Manvell notes the resemblance, here, to another artist Chaplin himself greatly admired:

> It would not perhaps be unfair to say that Chaplin has occupied much the same place in the hearts of the people of the twentieth century that Dickens occupied in the nineteenth, and that, because he was working in a new and internationalized visual medium, his public during the height of his success has been incomparably larger in numbers.[114]

Questionable, though, is which versions of his many works will be recognized as representative of his artistry. There have been many changes in titles, here and abroad, as Chaplin films have been bought or leased by distributors. Even Keystone sometimes changed the old titles when it reissued its films:

> The earlier films have been copied or "duped," cut, rearranged, and supplied with new subtitles, which tried distressingly to be funny. They have been provided with "grunts and whistles" and a bit of music on sound tracks which overaccelerate the action. In spite of the grave loss in quality, they can still open the door to delight.[115]

Recently, one of these doors was opened via the discovery of a long-lost Chaplin film score. In February 1994, *The Circus* was shown in New York at the Metropolitan Museum of Art; the score, performed by the Manhattan School of Music Chamber Sinfonia, had been discovered in 1992 in the archives at the family estate in Switzerland. This original score had been created under Chaplin's supervision decades earlier, to be played only by a live orchestra or pianist accompanying the film. The recent production was received with enthusiasm and delight from critics and audiences alike.

Eighty years after his creation, the Little Tramp is alive and kicking.

Notes

Introduction: A Tramp Is Born

1. Charles Chaplin, *My Autobiography*. 1964. Reprinted New York: Plume, 1992.
2. Chaplin, *My Autobiography*.
3. Frank N. Magill, ed., *Magill's Survey of Cinema: Silent Films*. Englewood Cliffs, NJ: Salem Press, 1982.

Chapter 1: A Dickensian Childhood

4. Roger Manvell, *Chaplin*. Boston: Little, Brown, 1974.
5. Quoted in Chaplin, *My Autobiography*.
6. Quoted in Chaplin, *My Autobiography*.
7. Quoted in Chaplin, *My Autobiography*.
8. Quoted in Chaplin, *My Autobiography*.
9. Quoted in Chaplin, *My Autobiography*.

Chapter 2: Learning His Craft

10. Manvell, *Chaplin*.
11. Chaplin, *My Autobiography*.
12. Quoted in Manvell, *Chaplin*.
13. Chaplin, *My Autobiography*.
14. Quoted in David Robinson, *Chaplin: His Life and Art*. New York: McGraw-Hill, 1985.
15. Quoted in Robinson, *Chaplin: His Life and Art*.
16. Quoted in Robinson, *Chaplin: His Life and Art*.
17. Manvell, *Chaplin*.
18. Raoul Sobel and David Francis, *Chaplin: Genesis of a Clown*. London: Quartet Books, 1977.
19. Quoted in Robinson, *Chaplin: His Life and Art*.
20. Quoted in Robinson, *Chaplin: His Life and Art*.
21. Quoted in Robinson, *Chaplin: His Life and Art*.
22. Dan Kamin, *Charlie Chaplin's One-Man Show*. Metuchen, NJ: Scarecrow Press, 1984.
23. Quoted in Robinson, *Chaplin: His Life and Art*.
24. Quoted in Robinson, *Chaplin: His Life and Art*.

Chapter 3: The First Year in Films

25. Quoted in Robinson, *Chaplin: His Life and Art*.
26. Manvell, *Chaplin*.
27. Quoted in Manvell, *Chaplin*.
28. Quoted in Manvell, *Chaplin*.
29. Eric Rhode, *A History of the Cinema: From Its Origins to 1970*. New York: Hill and Wang, 1976.
30. Quoted in Manvell, *Chaplin*.
31. Quoted in Gerald D. McDonald, Michael Conway, and Mark Ricci, eds., *The Films of Charlie Chaplin*. Secaucus, NJ: Citadel Press, 1965.
32. Quoted in Manvell, *Chaplin*.
33. Chaplin, *My Autobiography*.
34. Quoted in McDonald et al., eds., *The Films of Charlie Chaplin*.
35. Robinson, *Chaplin: His Life and Art*.
36. Rhode, *A History of the Cinema*.
37. Rhode, *A History of the Cinema*.
38. Chaplin, *My Autobiography*.

Chapter 4: The Most Famous Man in the World

39. Manvell, *Chaplin*.
40. Robinson, *Chaplin: His Life and Art*.
41. Quoted in Robinson, *Chaplin: His Life and Art*.
42. Robinson, *Chaplin: His Life and Art*.
43. McDonald et al., eds., *The Films of Charlie Chaplin*.

44. Joe Franklin, *Classics of the Silent Screen*. Secaucus, NJ: Citadel Press, 1959.

45. Quoted in McDonald et al., eds., *The Films of Charlie Chaplin*.

46. Robinson, *Chaplin: His Life and Art*.

47. Kamin, *Charlie Chaplin's One-Man Show*.

48. Quoted in Robinson, *Chaplin: His Life and Art*.

49. Quoted in Robinson, *Chaplin: His Life and Art*.

50. Quoted in Sobel and Francis, *Chaplin: Genesis of a Clown*.

51. Magill, ed., *Silent Films*.

52. Quoted in Sobel and Francis, *Chaplin: Genesis of a Clown*.

Chapter 5: Challenges of Art and Life

53. Chaplin, *My Autobiography*.

54. Chaplin, *My Autobiography*.

55. Robinson, *Chaplin: His Life and Art*.

56. Quoted in Robinson, *Chaplin: His Life and Art*.

57. Quoted in McDonald et al., eds., *The Films of Charlie Chaplin*.

58. Chaplin, *My Autobiography*.

59. Quoted in Jerry Epstein, *Remembering Charlie: The Story of a Friendship*. New York: Doubleday, 1989.

60. Chaplin, *My Autobiography*.

61. Quoted in McDonald et al., eds., *The Films of Charlie Chaplin*.

62. Quoted in Magill, ed., *Silent Films*.

63. Quoted in McDonald et al., eds., *The Films of Charlie Chaplin*.

64. Gerald Mast, *A Short History of the Movies*, 5th ed. New York: Macmillan, 1992.

65. Quoted in Manvell, *Chaplin*.

66. Quoted in McDonald et al., eds., *The Films of Charlie Chaplin*.

67. Quoted in McDonald et al., eds., *The Films of Charlie Chaplin*.

68. Manvell, *Chaplin*.

69. Quoted in Robinson, *Chaplin: His Life and Art*.

70. Manvell, *Chaplin*.

71. Quoted in McDonald et al., eds., *The Films of Charlie Chaplin*.

72. Quoted in Magill, ed., *Silent Films*.

73. Chaplin, *My Autobiography*.

74. Franklin, *Classics of the Silent Screen*.

75. Chaplin, *My Autobiography*.

Chapter 6: Social Issues

76. Chaplin, *My Autobiography*.

77. Quoted in McDonald et al., eds., *The Films of Charlie Chaplin*.

78. Manvell, *Chaplin*.

79. Chaplin, *My Autobiography*.

80. Quoted in Mast, *A Short History of the Movies*.

81. Quoted in Robinson, *Chaplin: His Life and Art*.

82. Quoted in McDonald et al., eds., *The Films of Charlie Chaplin*.

83. Chaplin, *My Autobiography*.

84. Chaplin, *My Autobiography*.

85. Chaplin, *My Autobiography*.

86. Chaplin, *My Autobiography*.

87. Manvell, *Chaplin*.

88. Chaplin, *My Autobiography*.

89. Chaplin, *My Autobiography*.

90. Quoted in McDonald et al., eds., *The Films of Charlie Chaplin*.

Chapter 7: Banishment and Return

91. Quoted in Robinson, *Chaplin: His Life and Art*.

92. Quoted in Manvell, *Chaplin*.

93. Quoted in Robinson, *Chaplin: His Life and Art*.

94. Quoted in Manvell, *Chaplin*.

95. Quoted in McDonald et al., eds., *The Films of Charlie Chaplin.*

96. Quoted in Manvell, *Chaplin.*

97. Quoted in Robinson, *Chaplin: His Life and Art.*

98. Quoted in Robinson, *Chaplin: His Life and Art.*

99. Quoted in Robinson, *Chaplin: His Life and Art.*

100. Quoted in Robinson, *Chaplin: His Life and Art.*

101. Quoted in Robinson, *Chaplin: His Life and Art.*

102. Quoted in McDonald et al., eds., *The Films of Charlie Chaplin.*

103. André Bazin, *Essays on Chaplin.* New Haven, CT: University of New Haven Press, 1985.

104. Quoted in Robinson, *Chaplin: His Life and Art.*

Epilogue: The Importance of Charlie Chaplin

105. Quoted in Robinson, *Chaplin: His Life and Art.*

106. Quoted in Bazin, *Essays on Chaplin.*

107. Quoted in Robinson, *Chaplin: His Life and Art.*

108. Sobel and Francis, *Chaplin: Genesis of a Clown.*

109. Quoted in Magill, ed., *Silent Films.*

110. Mast, *A Short History of the Movies.*

111. Bazin, *Esssays on Chaplin.*

112. Quoted in Bazin, *Esssays on Chaplin.*

113. Mast, *A Short History of the Movies.*

114. Manvell, *Chaplin.*

115. Quoted in McDonald et al., eds., *The Films of Charlie Chaplin.*

For Further Reading

André Bazin, *Essays on Chaplin*. New Haven, CT: University of New Haven Press, 1985. With a preface by acclaimed French film director François Truffaut, this small volume contains many challenging short essays on Chaplin by a prominent film critic. Especially entertaining is an essay on *The Great Dictator* that explains how, after Hitler "copied" Chaplin's mustache, Chaplin made the film to "take his mustache back" and ultimately destroy the image of the Nazi leader. No photos.

Dan Kamin, *Charlie Chaplin's One-Man Show*. Metuchen, NJ: Scarecrow Press, 1984. Dan Kamin is a working mime who studied and analyzed Chaplin's technique and discusses it from a technical point of view. This book goes a long way to help the reader understand how and why Chaplin created specific movements for his Little Tramp; this fascinating work is a guide to the art of Charlie Chaplin. Many revealing black-and-white photos, and a moving introduction by the great mime Marcel Marceau.

Frank N. Magill, ed., *Magill's Survey of Cinema: Silent Films*. Englewood Cliffs, NJ: Salem Press, 1982. The first in Magill's ambitious three-volume work, *Silent Films* includes a fine essay on Chaplin's short films, as well as other important writings on related topics, including "Costume Design in Silent Films" and "A Directorial History of Silent Films," which cover Chaplin's contribution. No photos.

Eric Rhode, *A History of the Cinema: From Its Origins to 1970*. New York: Hill and Wang, 1976. The author spent five years researching and writing this one-volume history of the cinema, and the hard work shows. This book is a feast for anyone searching for an introduction to the cinema. The entries on Chaplin, appropriately spread out over the length of the book, show Chaplin as a man shaped by his times and his peers. There are many interesting black-and-white photos, though only a few of Chaplin.

Neil Sinyard, *Directors: The All-Time Greats*. New York: Gallery Books, 1985. The author places Chaplin at the beginning of an impressive collection of portraits of famous and influential film directors. Many black-and-white photos, including several widely reproduced images of Chaplin.

Jerry Vermilye, *The Films of the Thirties*. Secaucus, NJ: Citadel Press, 1985. This book focuses on the decade that produced many great Hollywood films, including Chaplin's *City Lights* and *Modern Times*. Many black-and-white photos.

Additional Works Consulted

Liz-Anne Bawden, ed., *The Oxford Companion to Film*. New York: Oxford University Press, 1976. Bawden's work is a delightful compendium of cinema knowledge, worldwide in scope. It ranges in time from the silent movies to the mid-1970s and includes solid information not only on Chaplin and his films but on related subjects, including slapstick, Mack Sennett, and the introduction of sound in films. Some black-and-white photos.

Charles Chaplin, *My Autobiography*. 1964. Reprinted New York: Plume, 1992. This is the book to start with for those interested in the man who became the greatest comedian of all time. Chaplin, working from memory, offers plenty to savor, especially regarding the infancy of the film industry in Hollywood, and the political controversies that arose later in his life. However, the most moving remembrances are of his childhood in London. Black-and-white photos included, with captions by Chaplin.

Jerry Epstein, *Remembering Charlie: The Story of a Friendship*. New York: Doubleday, 1989. This book is a delightful and often revealing remembrance of a man who became an associate and a close friend of Chaplin near the end of Chaplin's long career. While the author provides commentary on much of Chaplin's life in films, Epstein is at his best describing their relationship and those he witnessed up close during Chaplin's later years in Switzerland. There are many fine black-and-white photos.

Joe Franklin, *Classics of the Silent Screen*. Secaucus, NJ: Citadel Press, 1959. Franklin, a long-time television personality in New York City, offers his recollections and opinions on many great silent films, including several by Chaplin. Many black-and-white photos, including a few of Chaplin.

Roger Manvell, *Chaplin*. Boston: Little, Brown, 1974. Roger Manvell, former director of the British Film Academy and a distinguished critic and lecturer, provides a fine thematic introduction to the life and work of Charlie Chaplin. Published in 1974, while Chaplin was still alive, the book seems incomplete compared to later works; however the writer's fine wit and historical perspective, as well as the inclusion of many excellent black and white photos, make up for the absence of material on Chaplin's last years and death.

Gerald Mast, *A Short History of the Movies*, 5th ed. New York: Macmillan, 1992. This book, widely used at the university level, offers a wealth of detailed, balanced, and accurate information about the history of the cinema from its inception up through the 1970s. Chapter Five is devoted to Mack Sennett and the Chaplin short films, placing both men in the context of the tremendous expansion of the movie industry during the years of World War I (1914–1918). There are a few photos of Chaplin.

Gerald D. McDonald, Michael Conway, and Mark Ricci, eds., *The Films of Charlie Chaplin*. Secaucus, NJ: Citadel Press, 1965. This book documents the film career of Charlie Chaplin. Each film is represented by two or three short reviews written at the time of the film's opening. There are also two fine introductory essays by editors McDonald and Conway, as well as numerous photos throughout.

David Robinson, *Chaplin: His Life and Art*. New York: McGraw-Hill, 1985. Having received permission from Oona Chaplin to use the Chaplin archives of private papers, records, letters, and photographs, film critic David Robinson produced what is widely regarded as the most complete and authoritative biography on Charlie Chaplin. This important and entertaining work includes a chronology, filmography, list of theater tours, list of important people in Chaplin's life, and eighty pages of black-and-white photos.

Raoul Sobel and David Francis, *Chaplin: Genesis of a Clown*. London: Quartet Books, 1977. This work has a British perspective, which may seem awkward to young American readers. But there is much of value here, including a discussion of the sources of the various bits of costume and mime that made up the "style" of the Little Tramp. There are moving descriptions of London—its poverty, its entertainments, its spirit—at the time of Chaplin's birth and youth, and the book includes obscure turn-of-the-century advertisements and other cultural artifacts that give the flavor of Chaplin's times, especially his childhood. There are also many wonderful black-and-white photos.

Index

Picture Credits

About the Author

Arthur Diamond is the author of several nonfiction books. Born in Queens, New York, he has lived and worked in Colorado, New Mexico, and Oregon. He received a bachelor's degree in English from the University of Oregon and a master's degree in English/Writing from Queens College. He lives in his boyhood home with his wife Irina and their children Benjamin Thomas and Jessica Ann.